MY TWEETS TO YOU

by

Eugene L. Moore,
Ph.D. Candidate

I0138527

Life To Legacy, LLC

My Tweets to You
© 2015 by Eugene L. Moore

ISBN-13 978-1-939654-51-9

Printed in the United States
10 9 8 7 6 5 4 3 2 1

Front cover design by: Treviante Brown

Published by: Life To Legacy, LLC
2441Vermont Street, #57
Blue Island, IL 60406
877-267-7477
Life2legacybooks@att.net

ABOUT THE AUTHOR

Eugene L. Moore is a current doctoral student in Education Policy, Organization and Leadership at the University of Illinois at Urbana-Champaign, where he has received both his master's and bachelor's in Human Resources and Communication respectively. Born and raised in Chicago, Illinois in a single parent home, he has witnessed firsthand the consequences of not having a quality education. Fortunately, he received a scholarship from the Daniel Murphy Scholarship Foundation to attend the prestigious Providence St. Mel School (PSM) located on Chicago's West Side, which for nearly forty years had 100% of its graduates accepted to four-year colleges and universities.

Upon graduating from PSM, he received a four-year scholarship to the University of Illinois from College Bound, which is currently in operation as Chicago Scholars. This program is aimed at providing needed resources to underserved high school students by giving them access to a quality educational experience.

Eugene attributes his success to his relationship with God, the influence of his mother, grandmother, mentors, teachers, and his inner determination to think beyond his circumstances. He prides himself on giving back and has contributed to various organizations and institutions committed to service, education, and health both domestically and globally. He established an annual scholarship at the University of Illinois, which bears the names of his mother and grandmother. However, his biggest contribution to service is the founding of the non-profit Assurance Creek Youth Program (ACYP) in 2012, where he serves as the President and Chief Executive Officer. ACYP is birthed out of his experiences with great mentors and excellent educational institutions. It is his hope that Assurance Creek Youth Program will become an organization that inspires youth to unlock the greatness that lives inside of them and reach their God-given potential.

Humble by nature, Eugene L. Moore is not interested in creating a spotlight that only highlights his accomplishments, but believes his greatest legacy will come from the success of those whom he has aimed to inspire.

ACKNOWLEDGEMENTS

My heavenly Father has orchestrated a life for me filled with boundless opportunities. For that, I say thank you.

My family serves as my inspiration to strengthen future generations. For that, I say thank you.

My mother, Diane Moore, has been an integral part in my success, from making sure my belt was neatly fastened to demanding that I spoke with great articulation and conviction. For that, I say thank you.

My mentors have served as great examples of success. Paul J. Adams III, Gary Caplan, Marc Grayson, Todd Grayson, Joel Massel, Samuel Mendenhall, Jim Murphy, John Russell, and Emmett Vaughn have provided their time, advice, and resources. For that, I say thank you.

My teachers provided a space for me to explore my intellectual inquisitiveness. Amanda Keroes and Sharon Mixon were beyond exceptional and exemplified the power of great teachers. For that, I say thank you.

Alfred Kentigern Siewers, Associate Professor at Bucknell University, encouraged me as an undergraduate student to pursue writing. For that, I say thank you.

James D. Anderson Gutgsell, Professor at University of Illinois, and Laurence Parker, Professor at University of Utah, were supporters of my desire to pursue my doctorate. For that, I say thank you.

Dr. Dennis Woods and Life to Legacy Books moved this project forward with diligence and compassion. For that, I say thank you.

Finally, there will always be people who you fail to acknowledge, but just because your name is not mentioned, that does not mean you are not appreciated for your understanding and encouragement. For that, I say thank you.

FOREWORD

It is difficult to grasp how messages of this magnitude could possibly be restricted by 140 mere characters. The author's ability to work within those boundaries to create endless profound thoughts is what makes this work an original and beautiful piece. *My Tweets to You* stretches the reader beyond the shallow surfaces of life and to a deeper place discovered by the author. He delves deep into the beauties of life, love, and success, while exploring their accompanying complexities.

I have witnessed Eugene L. Moore firsthand as he assess life situations and effortlessly articulates the profound lessons in it. Over the last couple of years, he began to preface his thoughts on life with the statement, "Now … that's a Tweet!" This compilation of his Tweets will leave the reader with a new outlook and a higher level of understanding.

Eugene's prolific writing and speaking abilities may have been heightened via his vast experiences in Corporate America and academia, however his thoughts are undoubtedly from a higher source. Eugene is conscious of his God-given talents and, as seen in this book, he can readily and effectively convey all that life entails in a constricted Tweet.

These powerful lessons are for people of all ages. If a chief purpose of Twitter is to follow and read another's message, then *My Tweets to You* is that and more!

—*Laurie June Samuels*
Attorney at Law
Chicago, Illinois

Presented To

Send Emails to:
info@assurancecreekyouth.org

PREFACE

Social media continues to be a driving force for businesses and individuals who desire a platform for their voices to be heard. Like in all things, there is good and bad in social media. Twitter, unlike other media outlets, restricts users to a 140-character limit, which for some makes it difficult to express their thoughts. However, when you enter a space with more than half a billion users, you decide whether you desire to add impact or simply be a part of the minutia that the space inherently creates. In *My Tweets to You*, I address broad subject matter ranging from success to failure to provide readers with concise yet provocative Tweets which speak to various life circumstances. The book features more than 1,200 Tweets. I hope each reader finds one that speaks directly to their situation.

LET THE TWEETS BEGIN

My Tweets to You

God is Awesome and we owe it to Him to reach our greatest potential.

Wrestling with man is a waste of time and effort. Why not wrestle with the one who wants to bless you? #WrestleWithGod

Although the situation seems unbearable, trust that God does His best work in the valley. #ValleyBlessings

A magnet cannot choose what it attracts but as humans, we must discern the sincerity of one's attraction.

Courage isn't only the ability to stand while others cowardly sit, but it's also the ability to walk away from situations of false comfort.

If you desire to be free, you must refuse to look backwards and have the courage to leave it all behind. #LeapToDestiny

God can do all things, but what He refuses to do is make you love Him. The best choice you'll ever make is to choose God. #HeChoseYouFirst

When someone bangs on your door, it's startling. God's knock isn't obtrusive, but quiet and steady. #HeIsKnocking

There have been many times when the challenges of life were too overbearing, but I learned to trust God. #HeCarriedMe

Triumph rarely asks why me but tragedy quickly asks why me. On the cross Jesus asked why me but ultimately said why not me? #NoMoreQuestions

I go inside darkness not because it's easy but because I desire to fly. What will be your sacrifice? #ButterflyEffect

I've come to expect criticism is inevitable & varying opinions are common, but greatness never stumbles in the face of adversity. #BringItOn

To many, my accomplishments have been remarkable but I'd freely give it all away to ensure God doesn't hide His presence from me. #TakeItAll

Education was a primary role of Jesus, and His disciples often called Him teacher. Today education is just as important. #EducationIsPower

It's important to place yourself in an atmosphere that produces knowledge. However, you must be willing to apply it. #KnowledgeCentral

Impatience and fear replace confidence with doubt, causing many to settle. No matter how long it takes, God always provides. #SoWhySettle

Where is your focus? Where are you using the greatest amount of energy? Failure comes from a lack of focus and wasted energy. #FocusIsMyFuel

Be thankful God has allowed your life to be filled with substance and joy. So many people are consumed with boredom. #HeControlsMySchedule

We all have relationships ranging from family to friendship, but the best & deepest relationships are those of intimacy. #GodDesiresIntimacy

One big obstacle to success is not having the courage to walk away from distractions that impede your ability to succeed. #LetItGo

My Tweets to You

I never perceived you as my enemy & truly considered you my friend. But once you showed me who you were, I had no choice but to go. #Goodbye

Gifts create excitement, as you're eager to see what's inside. God has placed a jewel as priceless as a diamond inside of you. #OpenYourGift

Making soup is a process, and while most of the ingredients are individually good, they become even better when they are together. #TeamSoup

I'd rather be a person of faith than someone of extreme doubt. Doubt suffocates your dreams and kills hope. It will happen. #FaithToBelieve

Chasing riches continues to be a race many people are eager to enter, but at what cost? Some will run so fast they'll pass God. #LoveOfMoney

Some are quick to pose for a selfie and post it online for all to see. But taking a selfie doesn't mean you see yourself. #TakeACloserLook

A best friend loves you when it's difficult, but undoubtedly will disappoint you on some level. God's love is unchanging. #HisPerfectLove

Being misunderstood can be frustrating but what causes even greater frustration is trying to explain yourself to those who refuse to listen.

Life has thrown every obstacle your way but your maneuvering has been flawless. Even in weakness you exhibited strength. #FaithToTheFinish

Vacations provide a break from the normal routine. Whether you board a plane or feel the breeze of the open road, you must escape. #MeTime

Laughter is my medicine and love is my vice. My only known allergies are excuses & blame. God's in control and I accept where I am. #IAmWell

You'll become exhausted if you try to make sense of the complexities of life. Instead, take rest in knowing God will make sense of it all.

If you were on a desolate island where food & water are scarce, would you survive? For many, life can feel like an island. #BeASurvivor

Friends listen with the desire to help. Enemies listen only to voice their criticisms, and have no desire to help. #SpeakingWithTheEnemy

Beauty's only skin deep. Jesus's face is superficial but His heart is supernatural. Unlike beauty, character never fades. #SeeBeyondSkin

A plane can take you around the world & a space shuttle can take you beyond earth. But no matter how far you travel there's no escaping God.

Janet Jackson coauthored "Funny How Times Flies When You're Having Fun." But even in extreme boredom, time doesn't wait. #TickTock

It's great to plan. But in our efforts to make the future more promising, we must not go ahead of God by overlooking today. #PresentHelp

My Tweets to You

Avoidance isn't courage. Anger isn't correction. Anxiety isn't comfort. Freedom comes when you face what needs fixing. #ProblemSolved

We live in a world that celebrates individual achievement, but some of the most successful people are modest about their accomplishments.

Beethoven was one of the most prolific composers of his era, but some of his greatest works were created in deafness. #GreatnessHasNoLimits

Many are reluctant to admit they have it. Some are even unaware they possess it. But privilege is something we all have. #PrivilegedSelf

Youth need many resources: great schools, communities, parents and mentors. But most of all, they need a chance to showcase their talent.

A great misuse of your time and resources is trying to help those who've made a decision to be prisoners of the past. #ReallocatingResources

Politics & religion are divisive, but love is a great force that can bring even the most intolerable & polarized together. #IdeologyOfLove

You can spend all your time trying to figure out what others are doing, or you can do what makes perfect sense—focus on yourself. #SeeYou

Arrogance aims to make others feel small, but true greatness aims to make others become great. #InspirationNotIntimidation #GreatnessAwaits

Recognition is not the desire of someone who is humble and committed to service. A true servant seeks validation from God. #HeknowsMyWork

Outbreaks lead to many measures, ranging from isolation to quarantine. Unfortunately, mediocrity has become an outbreak. #InfectedByAverage

If you wait long enough, God will silence your enemies by giving you immeasurable success. But don't be distracted by hate. #WaitForHim

Success is like a magnetic force, for it attracts all types of people: opportunists, enemies, contributors and allies. #KnowYourSurroundings

To know that God exists is one thing. To develop a personal relationship with Him is another, for all He desires is our love. #FatherlyBond

Beware of those who continually inquire about what is happening in your life, as their intentions are not always sincere. #SoWhyAreYouAsking

Can you find confidence in chaos? Can you obtain success in sadness? Can you seek love in lies? For many, these questions remain unanswered.

Organization is a key skill for success. It allows you to navigate roadblocks with ease by always having an alternate route. #GetOrganized

Money can buy the best medical team but not a cure. Fame creates notoriety but not happiness. Make no room for conceit. #AFalseSenseOfPower

My Tweets to You

Your presence is enigmatic. Your purpose is essential. Your plan is exciting. It's obvious that God reigns in your life. #TooBigNotToNotice

Allow your dreams to be fed with hope by having no appetite for fear. Most importantly, allow the present moment to fill you up. #IAmFull

During the day the sun follows you. At night the stars chase you. But if you desire to be caught by love, you must seek the Creator. #TryGod

Awake with excitement and enthusiasm, not because your life is without blemish but because you've been given another chance. #EmbraceTheDay

You can choose to follow the masses or the Master but know that the masses will ultimately cause you to go astray. #MassHysteria #MasterPlan

Despite efforts to give, some see you as a threat, not an asset. Consequently their actions restrict your ability to help. #AssetDenied

If you're going to preach, make sure you have a captive audience, as they're most likely to listen and change accordingly. #WillingToListen

Do you know it for yourself or do you need someone else to tell you? True love doesn't seek validation, nor does it boast. #LoveSpectacle

Why concern yourself with critics? They accused, questioned, and sentenced Jesus to death. Here comes my betrayer! #GreatnessUnderAttack

Waiting for your blessing can be frustrating but God uses that time to eliminate those who aren't worthy to stand alongside you in victory.

Are you clever or clear? Are you chastising or compassionate? Are you caring or corrupt? Are you cynical or considerate? #WhoAreYouToday

Technology has changed how we navigate the world, but it restricts stillness, as we've become accustomed to instant gratification. #BeStill

Schools test academic proficiency. Employers test performance. Friends test loyalty. Doctors test health. God tests our faith. #PassTheTest

Your closest friend can only take you so far. At some point, you must have the strength and courage to seek God for yourself. #WaitingOnYou

Who you were yesterday should be different from who you are today. Live life on the continuum of growth, productivity and change. #Evolve

Some are boastful and arrogant in their victory but bitter and blameworthy in their defeat. True winners are humble in winning and losing.

You can walk, jog or run, but whatever you do, be active. Inactivity leads to poor health. The first step is all it takes. #BodyTemple

A prideful or stubborn person suffers in silence and rejects all forms of help, whereas a wise person voices their need for help. #GodHelpMe

Your mind is brilliant. Your spirit is enlightening. But your body suffers from neglect. Visit the doctor, exercise and be well. #BodyTemple

There's nothing more mind boggling than seeing an adult who's cognitively competent but reacts to the truth as an adolescent child. #GrowUp

The irony about your critics is that it's your success that initiates their critique. Be thankful for their continual gaze. #OpenForCritique

The arrogant believe they're the smartest one in the room, not accounting for the fact that knowledge doesn't have a sole heir. #NotTooSmart

People who have a strong work ethic and persevere amidst challenges take issue with those who limit themselves to excuses. #NoTimeForExcuses

A person who desires to be great refuses to partner with mediocrity, knowing that such a partnership would only be average. #GreatPartners

It's not wise to invest in someone who quits, as it will prove to be a costly mistake. Quitters fail to be present in victory. #InvestWisely

Believing in God is awesome but if you don't believe in yourself, you'll lack the confidence to receive His blessings. #ConfidentCredentials

Life entails trouble, but it's this reality which allows one to interrogate their inner strength and tenacity. #OnlyTheStrongSurvive

Great leaders are burdened with an immense amount of responsibility, as they take full ownership of their success & failure. #NoExcuseLeader

Although revisiting the past is inviting and the present is difficult, I refuse to focus on yesterday, as it has no value. #NoNeedToLookBack

You know what needs to be done & realize the consequences of inaction, but allow others to distract you from priorities. #InterruptionOfSelf

July 4, 1776 the USA gained independence from Great Britain and we've celebrated ever since. Your independence is your freedom. #July4th

Nothing really falls on deaf ears, as life will eventually force you to take notice of the wisdom you so foolishly disregarded. #LifeLessons

Those who show up in your defeat are better than those who show up in victory. Success easily finds superficial support. #GetRealSupporters

An academic uses research. A performer uses a stage. A teacher uses a classroom. A lawyer uses a courtroom. #PlatformToSucceed #StandOnIt

Success attracts many onlookers, but what's odd is that the majority of people gathered are only there for selfish gain. #WhosWho

Your home, car, education, career, family, friends and all those things which bring you joy are a mere reflection of His favor. #SeeGodNotMe

For the most part, people are only able to scrutinize your persona. They're typically unaware of the totality of your existence. #SeeAllOfMe

My Tweets to You

Just because you claim to be unaware of the privilege you've been granted doesn't negate the fact you benefit from it #PrivilegedOne

Life's not a fairytale. It's equipped with hardships and unforeseen circumstances. But when you know Christ, you endure. #HisFairytaleEnding

How you respond to greatness is an indication of your ability to succeed. Some are jealous. Others are excited. #SuccessAdmiresGreatness

Where are your priorities? Are you focused on image or reality? Do you desire power or peace? How do you see yourself? #QuestionsNeedAnswers

The irony is that most people have some regrets but if they were given a chance to do it over they'd likely do it the same #ChangeOrRepeatIt

Arrogance believes ambition, talent & intelligence are the only factors for success, not realizing who orchestrates it all. #GodTheConductor

You stand on the broad shoulders of ancestors who prayed before you were born that greatness would forever be your reality. #HeHeardThem

Some people are unwilling to assist in the phases of planning and execution but are willing to help once success is achieved. #NoHelpWanted

The greatest lessons in life are found in tragedy, failure & rejection, for they force you to recover, persevere & win. #ItMakesYouStronger

Some people who aren't well physically, emotionally, or spiritually have the capacity to push their greatest supporter away. #BeWell

Curiosity & openness can take you on a journey to success, but close mindedness & indifference can lead to failure. #OpenlyCuriousToSucceed

Our time is limited but our existence is intentional. Ask yourself why you were born. There's a unique reason for your life. #BornForPurpose

Imitation only leaves room for you to occupy second place. For some, that's good, but allow your originality to be first place.

Nurture your own talents, not your critic's. They have no intentions to support your success. They stand on the outside of your greatness.

Your mentality has a greater impact than your positionality. Learn to see beyond your circumstances and strive to create new possibilities.

Although you have exhausted your options, you must have faith in God, knowing He will deliver & exceed your expectations. #CanYouSayOverflow

Intelligence appreciates. Ignorance depreciates. Undoubtedly, ignorance costs more, but intelligence has more value. #TheValueOfIntelligence

Hope comes in a faint whisper. Giving up comes in a resounding shout. You must quiet your surroundings or you'll succumb to the noise.

Youth can't allow deluded images of success to limit the depth of their dreams. You're far more dynamic than athleticism or vocal ability.

My Tweets to You

You interrogate me to uncover my flaws. You chastise me to expose my vulnerability. You demean me to unmask my insecurity. #YouFailed

What happens to a child born into poverty? Despite their eagerness to learn, it feels like a street without an outlet. #OpenTheRoadToSuccess

Don't allow fear to become your makeshift prison. Be fearless in your attempts to fulfill your goals by breaking out. #SuccessConquersFear

Some people are humbly longing for help, while others are reluctant and unappreciative when it's given. Who are you helping? #HelpMeHelpYou

Success spends no time dragging others to a higher level of understanding because it realizes those who desire greatness aren't resistant.

A misconception about success is that it's easy, but those who have it know it's a struggle to achieve & a fight to maintain. #ConstantWork

We all need someone to trust. But when you're tired of being disappointed by family & friends, know that God will provide. #UnexpectedAngel

Some people only see you as a resource and once you stop providing they'll quickly depart. Don't waste your resources on the undeserving.

Are you tired from dreaming or are you tired from working to make it a reality? Dreams are great but at some point, you awake. #MakeItHappen

Time has no loyalty and is often insensitive to our wants and needs. In light of this reality, we must maximize each moment. #NoTimeToLose

If success was located on the mountaintop, how far would you climb? If it was on the floor of the ocean, how deep would you dive? #WorkForIt

When we're most afraid, we can't succumb to the manipulation of fear because the moment we do, we relinquish hope. #InGodWhomShallIFear

The underdog is intriguing, not because others believe they're less likely to win, but because they persevere amidst the scrutiny. #WonItAll

God can heal a broken heart. He can fix those things which are shattered. He can restore what appears lost, but we must seek Him. #GoToGod

If you'd ask a successful person how many times they hear "no" or experience rejection, they'd instinctively say a lot. #NoBeforeYes

Wisdom isn't just what you know but what you're willing to share. Wisdom doesn't hoard knowledge or insight but gives to all. #WisdomToShare

Life has many roads and we must avoid those which cause us pain, sorrow & regret by not circling the same roads of despair. #TakeAnotherRoad

We all have limits but what makes us different is how we see them. Some enjoy living on the edge, while others play it safe. #KnowYourLimits

My Tweets to You

Some people believe they should only give when they've succeeded financially or socially, but such a notion is absurd. #GiveNowWhyWait

You've waited for a long time & frustration has begun to mount. But if you just hold on, you'll see the Helping Hand of God. #HopeInWaiting

When you compare yourself to others, you can feel insignificant. If you desire significance, you must fulfill your purpose. #PurposefulYou

You say you want more but you do less. You say you want to give but don't. You say you want the best but settle for the worst. #DoAsYouSay

If you're not careful, you'll define yourself through the invasive lens of others and minimize the most important perspective. #YouDefineYou

Personality, confidence & results are key factors in rating leadership. Great leaders continually develop their skills. #BecomeAGreatLeader

Everyone has an opinion but your mere entitlement doesn't make what you say more valid or true. Truth silences opinion. #TruthOrOpinion

You can't change what others think about you. The most beloved person has enemies. Silence them with your greatness and love. #BeAboveHate

At birth our life is somewhat of a blank page. As we get older, the writing process begins. Prewrite. Draft. Revise. Edit. Publish. #MyStory

A great mentor is someone who doesn't hesitate to make an investment in others, realizing the importance of giving back. #MentorsMatter

To be successful you must be your greatest critic. Be humble to understand you don't have all the answers and be willing to pay it forward.

A car runs on fuel and we have adrenaline to intensify our effort by maximizing our strength. Can you feel the Rush? #TheRushOfIntelligence

When God has orchestrated your waiting period, be assured your waiting will not be in vain. He will exceed your expectations. #WorthTheWait

Success cannot be confined to a box, nor is it content with what most consider good, but only seeks the best option. #GreatnessBreaksOut

A wise person never replaces those who got them there with those who found them there. Success comes with many fake friends. #BeLoyalToReal

Education is a doorway to success. But for many children, those doors are locked shut. Children & parents are loudly knocking. #OpenUpPlease

Noise redirects our focus. Hence, emergency vehicles have sirens. Clarity is found in the stillness of silence. #SilentFocus

You can spend your entire life trying to be what others think you should be or you can become the person God knows you can be #BeAllYouCanBe

My Tweets to You

Some people want you to believe your intelligence robs them of opportunity, but their jealousy is what restricts their options. #SeeYouNotMe

Nerds are socially attacked for their quirkiness but are economically rewarded for their brilliance. Popularity is relative. #NerdNation

When you needed strength, I was strong. When you needed advice, I was a counselor. When you needed comfort, I comforted. #AFatherProtects

Regret is like a thorn in your side. In an effort to live outside of this reality, you must make wise decisions. #ThinkBeforeYouDecide

Commonality is greater than differences Love is greater than hatred Forgiveness is greater than pain Pride is greater than shame #BeGreater

Change is most difficult when you're satisfied with your situation. But once you decide the familiar is unacceptable, change is inevitable.

I hadn't experienced it and just didn't understand it but once I became aware of it, I only had two options to ignore it or accept it. #Change

You weren't given eyesight to be blind, a voice to be silent or limbs to be motionless, but instead are called to see, speak & move. #DoIt

An insincere fan will celebrate your victory with exuberance, but the moment you lose, they'll be the first to express disdain. #FanOrFoe

Success isn't intimidated by the world stage, but aims to become the main attraction by working hard in the dark. #SpotlightOfSuccess

Some people will attempt to convince you they've lived without opportunities and encouragement. Perhaps their sentiments are true. #TryGod

They claim that you're toxic but instead of leaving, they desire more of you. Jealousy will always see you as a toxic addiction #FreeYourself

Don't tolerate hatred. Don't be blind to injustice. Don't be afraid to challenge the status quo. Have the courage to stand while others sit.

When tragedy comes, some people instantly find those who have a relationship with Christ. Perhaps you should develop one. #GoToHimYourself

You don't have it because you're not working hard to get it or God is saying, "Not now". Either way, you must do your part. #WorkForIt

Great leaders are accustomed to receiving feedback. Instead of being defensive or arrogant, they listen and decipher what is useful. #GotIt

When you love humanity, you refuse to clothe it in race, color, ethnicity, gender, or anything that disrupts its continuity. #WeAreOnePeople

Only "the can'ts" say you can't. Refuse to listen to those who doubt your ability based on their lack of capability. #CanDoWillDoAlreadyDone

My Tweets to You

If you desire clarity, you must eliminate the noise of negativity & surround yourself with the silence of greatness.
#FeelItHearItSeeItBeIt

Don't feel diminished by defeat but be determined to fulfill your dreams & endure the obstacles that precede winning.
#VictoryWithinMyReach

Words are powerful and we must use them cautiously, with an intentionality that intensifies love, hope and unity.
#WordsToLiveBy

Success is like finding ancient fossils or diamonds. They are rarely discovered on the surface, but you must explore the deep.
#DigForIt

You'll never find the basement occupying the penthouse. To succeed, surround yourself with people on and above your level.
#NextLevel

If you live long enough you'll make mistakes but the lessons gained should always outweigh the consequences.
#MistakesCostlyLessonsPriceless

Poet Maya Angelou once said, "When you know better, you do better." Once you know better, fight to make this statement true.
#DoBetterToday

Great memories are birthed from great moments, for life encompasses so much uncertainty you can quickly become distracted.
#MyMomentToShine

If someone is content with eating hamburgers, don't waste your time trying to convince them what they're missing in filet mignon.

Most children love superheroes, as their imagination soars higher than Superman, wider than Spiderman, and faster than Batman. #ImagineThat

Listening is essential to success. If you fail to listen you'll make unnecessary mistakes with no guarantee of recovery. #ListenToSucceed

The past can't be altered and the future can't be created so the only hope for change is today. Why are you waiting? #ChangeItUp

A resolution is hardly ever reached in silence, but is gained through consensus or compromise using constructive communication. #TalkAboutIt

History is a road map that unlocks potential & allows you to reach further, with the hope you'll leave a greater history to explore. #KnowIt

Everyone has a story and each one varies. But the challenge lies in not defining yourself by one story. #CreateMoreChaptersForTheBookOfYou

Never settle or become satisfied with being someone you're not, but have the courage to be the best possible you. #DiscoverYourGreatness

Fear motivates cruelty and intensifies hatred, whereas courage inspires kindness and encourages love. My courage is my strength. #FearNot

A tiger has excellent night vision, giving them an advantage over their unsuspecting prey. Your vision marks your success. #EyeOfTheTiger

Relationships are many things but mostly they're a demonstration of being there when it matters most. Spouse partner family friend. #BeThere

"Don't judge a book by its cover" implies that you should read the entire book to make the best assessment. #WisePeopleLearnToSkim

Before you aimlessly seek to satisfy your desires, be sure to account for the consequences your actions will cause. #TheCostOfDisobedience

Success can't be purchased, but failure has a price. To be paid by success you must be willing to work. What's your compensation? #WorkForIt

A true partner doesn't bashfully walk behind nor do they boastfully walk in front, but boldly walk in step. #PartnersWalkTogether #GetInLine

You can't find it looking backwards nor will a crystal ball assist you in discovering it, for NOW can only be found in the present moment.

In an effort to be seen some people clothe themselves in fakeness. Society focuses on the external. But God sees the internal. #TheRealYou

Legendary woman, poetic genius, prolific writer, artist, motivational speaker, activist, professor, & friend—Maya Angelou. #SheStillRises

Life is just as fluid as the ocean's waves and swift as the nature's wind, but you must be able to handle the transitions. #BraceYourself

Examine your motives before going full force into a new endeavor. You might discover your intentions aren't sincere. #DoItForTheRightReason

How can you expect to be limitless when you consciously surround yourself with people who are so limited? Let go of the baggage. #FlyHigher

Undoubtedly, grandparents create a legacy and foundation for generations. But we must provide our own bricks of opportunity. #BrickByBrick

To be successful you must have a high tolerance for hearing "no" and be willing to figure out many things on your own. #Persevere

Some people waste an enormous amount of time and energy on unrealistic goals but it's imperative to shift your focus. #AchieveRealisticGoals

While in Cleveland, Lebron James was criticized for his inability to win a championship, but now he has two titles. #ProveYourCriticsWrong

You can spend your entire life searching for love, but until you experience God's love, you'll always feel empty & incomplete. #NoSubstitute

Time is our greatest resource but we foolishly invest in those who are unwilling to provide a return on our investment. #RecoverYourLosses

Danger is real, yet soldiers bravely sacrifice their lives for our freedom. Their commitment is our greatest weapon. #WeSaluteYou

Had He given it to me when I wanted it, I wouldn't have been capable of sustaining it. But I patiently waited on His timing. #TheRightTime

Some U.S. cities are warzones, where youth are more inclined to defend themselves with bullets than books. #PovertyAndInjusticeBirthViolence

Education is the greatest tool to fight injustice. Without it, you're left to understand justice through the lens of the unjust. #MindPower

Militaries around the world are equipped with some of the most dangerous weapons but they give a false sense of protection. #GodProtectUsAll

NBA Playoffs is an exciting time. Whether your team is the Heat, Pacers, Spurs or Thunder, you can't deny the competitive edge. #PlayToWin

Most people are impressed with the accomplishments of others, but their greatest interest lies in knowing how they did it. #IWantToKnowHow

Some people find it illogical to make the bed daily but perhaps the logic lies in knowing you started your day with order. #ReadyForTheDay

Typically men enjoy sports, women enjoy shopping, and children enjoy playing. We must take pleasure in life without regret. #EnjoyYourself

Just because it's routine, comfortable and familiar doesn't mean you shouldn't challenge yourself to explore new possibilities. #ChangeItUp

You can spend your entire life defending your mistakes or you can avoid regret by accepting responsibility for your actions. #NowIKnowBetter

How you utilized the past moment provides insight into how you will behave in the present. The future will reflect your decisions. #YouDidIt

Gray is an intermediate color between white & black, but isn't considered a favorable color, as it's associated with dullness. #BrightenItUp

Failure rationalizes its results by believing it never had a chance to win but success always believes winning is possible. #ConfidenceToWin

Some people are allergic to truth and if it's spoken nicely or sternly, they reject it, as they can't handle its known side effect: CHANGE.

If you enjoy seeing the rainbow adorn the sky, you must welcome the rain. The storms of life eventually pass but we must hold on. #WaitForIt

Chronic complainers aren't solution oriented. They spend all their time talking about the problem without offering solutions. #TalkSolution

Sometimes our biggest obstacles are not due to a lack of understanding, but our inability to do what we know to be right. #DoTheRightThing

If we lived each day as if it were our last what would it entail? Hopefully we would embrace the present moment with love. #LastDayToLove

As a child, life is one big game, as you haven't been introduced to the stress of responsibility. But as an adult, the game ends. #GameOver

Some people who are unhappy spend their time focusing on others, as opposed to channeling their energy on themselves. #HappyToFocusOnMyself

Let's Make a Deal is based on the premise of making deals, with the understanding you might lose everything. Don't live your life by chance.

If you're not feeling well, are you likely to seek comfort from your family & friends or will you seek the comfort of God? #FindComfortInHim

Ironically, you can be surrounded by many people & still feel alone, or you can be in an empty room & feel crowded. #WithGodYouAreNotAlone

A giraffe and a tortoise occupy the same space but don't share the same view. Hence, we see the world from different views. #WhatDoYouSee

Everyone lives their life at a certain rotation. If their center is failure, then why are you entertaining their ways? #RotateAroundSuccess

Energy cannot be created or destroyed but those who choose to live a life of negativity will destroy their chances to experience true peace.

What you convey with your words will always be overshadowed by your actions. Limit the talk and focus on the doing. #DoSomethingBesidesTalk

How you treat others when you're on the top might determine how life will treat you when you've fallen. #LifeIsSubjectToChangeWithoutNotice

It takes humility and courage to accept mistakes, as it requires you to eliminate excuses and blame from your explanation. #OwnYourMistakes

It's great to have admiration for celebrities. Their fame can be captivating, but a more productive use of time is self-improvement. #SeeYou

When you have problems, it feels like you're on an island. But the reality is you're not the only one. We all have problems! #NoPityParty

Perhaps you believe it's you against the world but the greatest contender you will ever face is yourself. #KnockYourselfOut

Life happens, and consequently we will experience some level of misfortune. But we must not add to it by making poor decisions and excuses.

You can see the stars in the sky, the waves in the ocean & the mountain peaks. But imagine if you truly see your beauty. #HisAmazingCreation

Future effort is meaningless when you make a conscious decision not to embrace the present opportunity of today. #LiveLifeInTheNow

The message of success is clear. You must work as if it's your last chance, and if you should happen to fail, try harder. #LastChanceEffort

My Tweets to You

It's okay to say no but it's not okay to say yes to everything. If you're not careful people will abuse your yes & chastise your no. #SayNo

Our lives are a mere reflection of our collective decisions, whether they're good, bad or indifferent. #DecideWithCaution

Believe in something greater than yourself, as we all will leave this earth with unanswered questions. But never question the power of love.

The unknown boy gives two fish and five loaves. Generosity is not about quantity but sincerity. Give what you can and God will do the rest.

Wikipedia defines philanthropy as love of humanity, but we often equate it to rich people giving to charity. #JesusThePhilanthropist

The more difficult the challenge, the more courageous you must become. What appears impossible is only possible by effort. #GoBeyondPossible

A mother's story is special as she loves unconditionally, protects fiercely, sacrifices willingly and teaches constantly.

A side mirror has an inscription which reads "objects in mirror are closer than they appear," which implies distortion. #LookAheadForClarity

It's not advantageous to admire, flirt or mingle with, or date mediocrity. The longer you partner with average, the more average you'll be.

How quickly you give up is an indication of your level of success, as those who accomplish their goals exhibit great tenacity. #FinishIt

If your greatest accomplishment is watching others succeed, then chances are you haven't reached your full potential. #SpectatorOfSuccess

An algebraic equation is $2x+5=15$, where $x=5$. Success$=xy+z$. X is you. Y is God. Z is opportunity. What variable are you missing? #SolveIt

The first mistake is not trying and the second is to start and not finish. Imagine if pyramid builders quit prematurely. #PyramidOfSuccess

The road to success is filled with detours, delays and construction, but you must overcome these obstacles if success is your destination.

Miners have a dangerous job, but in the face of danger, their effort is supported by purpose. Why are you digging? #DigPurpose

To be extraordinary requires a great deal of sacrifice, an immense amount of effort & the perseverance of a lion on the hunt. #WhyBeOrdinary

Your desire to succeed shouldn't be about having what someone else has but about developing your own individual brand. #BrandOfSuccess

We have planners, but despite our attempt to bring organization to our lives, we must always be prepared for the unexpected. #AlteredPlans

My Tweets to You

Initially your frustration was confusing, as my love and loyalty were undeniable. But I learned your greatest frustration is you. #YouNotMe

People face the day with mixed emotions, ranging from anxiety to excitement. But regardless of your emotions find contentment. #ImGoodImHere

A person who is truly great at multitasking can do several things simultaneously without compromising quality. #AlwaysExpectMyBest

You can demand people listen to you or you can allow your actions to speak. I hear what you're saying but I see what you're doing. #ISeeYou

You were born into a unique family, one of strengths and weaknesses, one of joys and disappointments, but one created by God. #WeAreFamily

Dive headfirst into work, but immerse yourself in life. Don't drown in work, but bathe in life. #LivingBeyondWork

What happens when a 7-game series is tied 3-3? The choice is clear: win or go home. At times life seems to offer the same option. #PlayToWin

Friendship is best tested when you're in need. That's when you discover the vulnerability or strength of the relationship. #FriendshipTest

A farmer would be considered absurd if he wants to produce a crop without planting seed. Your lack of effort stops your growth. #PlantASeed

Not everyone has a published autobiography that chronicles their famed life but we're all innately writing our stories daily. #MyUntoldStory

The motivation and methods are likely to change but the message of success remains the same, which is one of hard work. #GetTheMessage

We all have gifts, but life's swift transitions can distract us from discovering our God given talents. #UnwrapAndShareYourGiftsToday

Why partner with someone who is content with being average and lacks confidence? Don't confuse helping with partnership. #PartnersOfSuccess

Historically previous generations have been concerned about the current youth, but concern is now an understatement. #DontLoseHope

Single people boast about their perceived freedom. Married couples complain about the lack thereof. We all have freedom to love. #TryLove

What is your motivation? What is your strategy? What are your intentions? These are questions from the heart. #AllowWisdomToInfluenceEmotion

I forgive for it provides me peace, but I remember because it provides me protection from being hurt by a repeat offender. #ForgiveNotForget

Intelligence is measured in many ways, but schools are convinced the best way is to use standardized tests, despite conflicting research.

Great comedians take what is seemingly controversial or painful, bring laughter to the audience, and for a moment, we escape. #LaughALittle

If your goal is to play it safe then opportunities which require some level of risk will always be outside of your reach. #ReachFurther

When undergoing certain tests, patients are required to fast beforehand to ensure accuracy, implying that preparation is key. #DoYourPart

If you spend all your money buying things you think you want, you will soon discover you no longer can afford what you really want. #NoMoney

If all you can handle is the sunshine, you will become vulnerable to the storm. Don't let the storms of life steal your joy. #StormChaser

Who you are when no one is looking is your truest self, as you're unfiltered. But what happens when there's a contradiction? #Exposed

Despite your efforts & desired outcome, you fell short of your goal. However failure coupled with effort isn't truly failure. #WinningEffort

Success knows it isn't personal and doesn't try to convince others it is but instead moves on to the next opportunity with more wisdom #Next

The popular saying "if it's meant to be, it will be" is somewhat misleading. It fails to indicate we can get in our own way of opportunity.

Some people live their lives in such a rush and despite accomplishing their goals, they rarely take time to enjoy success. #EnjoyTheMoment

René Descartes stated, "I think, therefore I am." To quote a genius doesn't make you a genius. If you desire to be a force of greatness be an original.

Your disposition of kindness, generosity & compassion will unfortunately create some enemies but it will create more allies. #KindlyGiveLove

It's wise to put your best foot forward but the greater level of wisdom is knowing you're headed in the right direction. #ThinkStepThinkStep

Some people have a dream and soon realize they should have been more thoughtful in their dreaming process. #DreamBiggerThanYourSurroundings

Some people have great desires and/or goals, but exert little to no effort in accomplishing them. Make it happen today! #MyEffortToAchieve

Don't create distance and wonder why you aren't close. It takes effort to build & demolish relationships. What's your construction project?

Fear and doubt become cowards in the face of adversity. Courage and hope become great warriors aimed at overcoming obstacles. #BraveHeart

You can feel estranged, isolated and distant from those you love. But ask yourself what you did to create the distance. #AskedForRoomToGrow

My Tweets to You

Your longing for perfection & superficial desires will cause you to sit on the steps of your home wondering why you're alone. #LoveNotLists

Being indecisive can be costly. Not knowing what you desire has an ultimate price tag of time, which cannot be replenished. #KnowWhatYouWant

If the ambiance of a restaurant is great but the food and service are lacking how likely are you to return? #QualityOverImage

Sometimes what we think we know contradicts what we actually know. It's okay to admit you don't know something, as no one knows everything.

It's imperative to be wise when selecting your team. My selection isn't personal or practical but purposeful. #ChooseYourTeamWisely

The seesaw, merry-go-round & swing are on many playgrounds, but where are the kids? On their computers, phones & game systems. #BeActive

Although crayons are inanimate objects, they represent the need for diversity. To enjoy the range of colors, you must include them all.

A marathon represents the collective & the individual. While we're all gathered in the same place, our rationale for participating differs.

What is it about you that incites their curiosity? Maybe your education, immense accomplishments or perhaps your notoriety. #GodInsideMe

Obstacles reveal your true intentions and level of determination. Success isn't easy so the question remains: how bad do you really want it?

If you haven't completed your goal, don't feel defeated, as you're closer than ever before. Just press forward and finish it. #WhyGiveUpNow

Don't become a follower of doubt or a crazed fan of fear. Instead be a leader of hope and a fanatic of faith and watch God change things.

If you truly want people to follow Christ, then be slow to judge & quick to love. An unloving Christian is a disappointing oxymoron. #BeLove

If you were suddenly awakened from the perfect dream, would you hasten back to it or would you be energized to make it a reality?

We become creatures of habit but once someone exits your life who added no intrinsic value, you'll eventually forget they left. #DontMissYou

It's important to forgive, as it represents compassion & wisdom. But what hinges on stupidity is allowing your enemy to control your actions

Young people understand opportunity comes to those who actively seek it, not to those who believe success is a lucky coincidence. #SeekIt

Who is jealous of poverty, mediocrity or failure? Therefore, don't be upset by their envy, as they're only responding to your success.

My Tweets to You

Some prestigious jobs require a selection committee prior to hiring a candidate, which implies a need for consensus. #StrategicPartnerships

A child awakes with joy and doesn't have any concerns, not because the world is without concern, but because it's of no consequence. #TryJoy

If you've come to a point in your relationship or career where you realize there is simply nothing to learn, gain, or give, then leave. #Now

Patience is a great attribute, but it's easier to wait on someone who's getting ready as opposed to someone who's not. #DontWaitForNothing

It's easy to demonstrate faith during success. The difficulty lies in your ability to demonstrate faith during failure. #FaithInFailure

It's important to understand failure often times comes before success & those who achieve it demonstrate perseverance. #TheProcessOfSuccess

It's great to have independence and the freedom to choose, but even your greatest choice isn't better than God's plan for you. #LetHimChoose

Imagine sitting in a waiting room where most of the people are sick, but in spite of it all they're filled with joy. #GuessImBetterThanILook

For some, heaven is a mythical place, but I wonder did people believe in the moon prior to Neil Armstrong and Apollo 11. #HeavenIsReal

It's said that as you get older you are less likely to suppress your opinions, even when they aren't politically correct. #TruthInYears

A lion's roar is used as a decoy to send prey away from the roar and straight into the trap of his pride. Fear can be deadly. #FearNot

What happens when you have a smartphone and a novice user? You not understanding the functionality doesn't diminish it. #IAmWhoIAm

Living in the past is different from reflecting on it. Reflecting on moments of joy and lessons learned will improve the present. #NoRepeats

Hospitals and churches have something in common: people who need help. Don't let the disposition of a few prevent you from getting help.

One of the many challenges of life is uncertainty. We have no control of what each day entails but we have the comfort of God. #CertainInGod

A great recipe is useless if you won't get the ingredients and follow directions. The recipe for success is hard work and sacrifice. #TryIt

Jealousy is hurtful. It can be hard to imagine that those close to you have such feelings, but jealousy is a side effect of insecurity.

Don't allow your life to become the next unsolved mystery. You were created with purpose but it's your job to execute a plan. #MysterySolved

My Tweets to You

You can't live life in reverse, nor is it wise to fast forward to the future, but the best option is to live in the moment. #PressPlayToday

Some people are cunning and use deception to advance their agenda. Others are clever in their approach, using intelligence. #YouTooClever

If you desire love, you must give love. For those who have given love but lack reciprocity, don't be disheartened, for love always prevails.

The art of war is strategic but the art of peace is equally strategic and always has a better outcome. #PeaceAmongNations

If schools were car dealerships and success was based on car sales, how massive a lot would we need? #AcresOfOpportunity

Problems come to the rich & poor. Tragedy attacks the strong & weak. Life isn't easy, but having peace and joy makes it easier. #PeacefulJoy

The disciples were afraid. But once He showed them His scars, they were no longer afraid. #LookAtMyHands #VictoryOfScars #ScarTestimony

You can't change anything by having excuses for everything. Blaming others for your mistakes exempts you from responsibility. #BlameExcuses

Though my friends betray me, deny they know me, beg for my public suffering, and attempt to kill me, still I rise. #Resurrection

Friday represents payday for some and the start of the weekend for most, but over 2000 years ago, the earth shook as Jesus died. #GoodFriday

Life is an endless book, and if you spend your time trying to create a perfect ending you'll miss all of the good chapters. #ThePlotThickens

Once you've compromised your reputation, money or fame can't easily repair it. You must use wisdom to guide your actions. #SacredReputation

Sometimes you can want more for a person than they desire for themselves. While this seems admirable, it creates frustration. #WastedEnergy

Although the journey is undeniably tough, the current moment isn't so bad. Today is good. Focus on His mercy and strength. #HeCarriesYou

Some people are quick to say something is too hard or too emotionally taxing. Unfortunately they're the ones who do nothing. #DoSomething

Your procrastination and lack of effort have proven to be unproductive. But your self-imposed obstacle is not my emergency. #No911

Misunderstanding history brings a high probability of making foolish mistakes. Learn from those who came before you. #WhatDoesHistoryTellYou

The Venom GT is the world's fastest car, which goes from 0 to 60mph in 2.7sec with a verified speed of 270.49mph. #UnlikeCarsLifeIsNotARace

God has plans for you, a future filled with hope. Your past no longer controls your present or future. #GreatExpectations

My Tweets to You

Successful people live on the outskirts of assumptions and quickly admit when something is outside of their expertise. #MakeNoAssumptions

Tradition is good but sometimes it outweighs common sense, as the typical response is, "We always do it this way." #NewWaysOfThinking

Life is no different than a construction zone. If you fail to adhere to the warning signs, you place yourself in grave danger. #SafetyFirst

You can become so comfortable living a life of lies, that the truth seems unnatural. But at some point, the truth is inescapable. #TheTruth

You can disguise unhappiness with a fake smile or clothe it with designer apparel, but true happiness is attainable. #GodIsHappiness

How you see yourself can differ from what others perceive. But as long as you strive to do your best, their perception carries little value.

Servants aren't concerned with rewards, recognition or repayment, but deliver service without expectation. #ServingYouWhileServingGod

Our dreams sometimes feel like a missing puzzle piece. Don't be discouraged. Eventually you'll find where the piece fits. #CompletePuzzle

A job is different from a career, as most jobs only provide earnings but careers provide opportunities for mobility. #CareerOverDeadEndJob

Manipulate it, procrastinate in it, take it for granted, embrace it, reflect on it, waste it, or maximize it, but you can't buy it. #Time

Time is irreplaceable, which makes every second sacred. Don't misinterpret my actions for insincerity or arrogance, but me maximizing time.

When we're moving we pack and eventually unpack, for we realize the value and necessity of what's inside each box. #UnpackHisLoveJoyAndPeace

My disposition isn't tied to accolades or material things, but solely to God. He is my ultimate joy. His love makes each day great. #GodInMe

Although I feel weak, my enemy is weaker. The pressure is strong but my faith is stronger. God is my strength & provider. #BoldUnderPressure

You can wait for a future moment of excitement which you have no guarantees you'll be present for, or you can embrace today. #NowIsTheTime

Leaders constantly face daily obstacles but they are strategic and progressive in their approach and thinking. #AlwaysReadyForTheChallenge

Crying over something you can change is a waste of time. Perhaps you can redirect your energy from tears and blame to action. #CryToChange

Trouble can cause the most rebellious person to listen, as they finally realize no amount of manipulation can stop their pain. #IAmListening

Your outlook isn't based on outward perception but inward perspective. See beyond your periphery & deeper than your frontal vision. #SeeMore

If you dropped your diamond ring in the trash, how willing would you be to search for it? God has placed greatness on the inside. #DigForIt

Those who lack a strategic element in their thinking are more likely to lose resources, as they aimlessly move forward without planning.

You can have a position of weakness within your circumstances or you can choose to have strength and defeat your obstacles. #StrongForBattle

It's virtually impossible to be a great leader if you can't control your emotions. Leaders seek the best solutions, not just consensus.

People travel all around the world to see the Statue of Liberty. But statues are motionless. As humans, we must not live life as statues.

Some of the most coveted jobs require extensive training. God uses our troubles as training but like the aspiring doctor, we must welcome it.

If you're not careful, your greatest strength can become your downfall because you've applied it to the wrong situation. #StrengthToMaintain

Let your situations become your sanctuary, not your struggle. Learn to embrace your situations, knowing God will provide a breakthrough.

Your past shapes how you see or perceive your future. However, despite the realities of the past you must see a future free of old mistakes.

You must never worship your own strength, talent or abilities, as you will quickly learn you are more limited than you think. #StrengthInGod

God isn't a magician, butler or maid aimed at satisfying your every selfish desire. He demands a faithful relationship that isn't one-sided.

Be engaged in the process if you desire victory. Faith without working hard is no more than a pipe dream of wishes. #TotalEngagement

Do you see God in your situation or are you too consumed by the magnitude of it all? God is bigger than anything you'll ever face. #ISeeYou

If you desire a clear focus, rid yourself of the self-imposed cloudiness that comes from focusing on others. Focus on yourself. #20/20Vision

Look up and see mesmerizing stars. Look down and see the fallen leaves of autumn. Look across and see the endless ocean. #CreationInMotion

The people you're surrounded by are an indication of your success. Don't hang out with average if you want to be great. #CircleOfSuccess

You might think I've got it all, but I worked for it all. Success isn't lazy, jealous or distracted by others, but strives to achieve.

My Tweets to You

If you don't have a relationship with God, your dependence will be on man, which will result in disappointment. #ReliableGodUnreliableMan

Successful people who deem themselves as risk-takers have no loyalty to fear, and neither should Christians. Fear is not of God. #NoFearHere

Some people won't like, agree with, or support you, and only serve as your opposition. But that's okay, as you never sought their approval.

Some people are tired from a wild night of partying. Some are exhausted from trying to find solutions to complex issues. #HangoverOrHistory

The politics of education creates chaos in a sacred space that should be free from unnecessary distractions. Change the focus #ChildrenFirst

I questioned the sincerity of your tears and high emotions because once the tears dried up, you reverted to your selfish ways. #CryToAction

Money can't buy it. Fame can't secure it. The strongest army can't defeat it. Material things can't replace it. #HappinessIsAGiftFromGod

There are many phrases in the Bible but the one that creates the greatest sense of unity, love and compassion is, "Our Father." #WeAreFamily

You prayed for transportation, I provided. You prayed for shelter, I provided. You prayed for healing, I provided. #NeverForgetWhatGodDid

In the beginning, you overruled my faith with your facts, but He has answered my prayers and disproved your expert opinion. #PrayerIsMyFact

When the odds are against you, you need to increase your faith. Despite the situation, I'm unbreakable, unshakable. #GodIsUnstoppable

Be willing to allow people to help you, knowing that it's in your humility that God will provide both His grace and mercy. #GodSendMeAnAngel

He was betrayed, falsely accused, beaten, denied and nailed to a cross stained by His Blood to save humanity. #StruggleSacrificeResurrection

My kindness is a given but loyalty is earned. It's foolish to be loyal to your enemies, as they clamor for your demise. #KindToAllLoyalToFew

One expects an auto shop to have cars which need repairs, as the exterior indicates what you'll likely find on the inside #ExteriorExpectations

Roadside Assistance is extremely convenient. It gives motorists an added sense of safety. But in order to get help you must call. #CallJesus

If my greatest flaw is being too optimistic, encouraging or just plain joyful then I'll take it, for I've never seen the righteous forsaken.

Worry & fear are siblings, but as a person of God, make a conscious effort to distance yourself from that side of the family. #NotRelated

Cars crash and sometimes the damages aren't repairable. But God didn't make cars in His image; He created man in His image. #NotEasilyBroken

A Christian should have an attitude of victory and blatantly reject failure because they will always have Jesus on their team. #SureVictory

A CAT scan can detect the abnormalities of organs and tissues but it fails to detect that Jesus lives inside of me. #InconclusiveResults

The battle inside your mind is the greatest one you'll ever face, but to win, you must stop fighting outside distractions. #InsideFocus

Know without equivocation that you're a child of a King, wonderfully & beautifully made. Boldly wear your crown & royal attire. #ChildOfGod

Christians have to experience loss, tragedy and defeat. But it's their resolve that indicates their trust in Him. #YourCrossYourResurrection

The time has come to decide whether to have a disposition of fear or faith. The only way to understand faith is by testing it. #PassTheTest

God loves the healthy & sick, the rich & poor, the educated & dropout, the one who makes it & the one who doesn't. #HeLovesYouAlways

You can count on people but unfortunately they'll let you down, not because they have ill will but because they're human. #CountOnJesus

We can choose our friends but God selects our family. Therefore, don't quarrel and harbor resentment, but love God's choice.
#LoveFamily

Your grip is so intense you're suffocating. You feel breathless, as your problems seem unbearable. Let go & let God handle it.
#BreatheAgain

An illusionist's skills are based on deception yet people are amazed by their acts. True amazement comes from God.
#MiracleWorkerNoIllusions

March Madness leaves little to the imagination concerning what it entails—the madness of the brackets, upsets & victories.
#EnjoyTheMadness

We place money in the stock market and it crashes. We put our faith in man and are disappointed. We gamble and lose.
#GodIsTheBestInvestment

When God blesses us, we must not become complacent in thankfulness or reflection but allow it to become a life lesson.
#ThankfullyReflective

It's important to stand in agreement. The Bible says when two or more agree on earth, it is done by the Father in Heaven.
#WeAgreeItsDone

In nursing homes, hospitals, and our homes, we have caregivers. While we fervently pray for the patient, we must not forget the caregivers.

There are multiple ways to one destination but the way of the Lord only has one path. Are you headed in the right direction?
#JesusTheOneWay

My Tweets to You

I believe in the Son, not just the sunset. I am bold about my love for Jesus. I pay taxes and tithes. Faith embodies my actions. #IBelieve

The doctor's report wasn't good. But I had to tune out the noise of those who foreshadowed my demise and listen for God. #IAmHealed

You can choose to worry about everything and solve nothing or you can pray about everything and experience God's truth. #PrayerKeepsMeAlive

Kindness doesn't seek recognition but shows one's ability to give to those who least expect it. Kindness is truly a gift. #PayItForward

The community is in an uproar and a town hall meeting has been scheduled, but the seats are empty. #CouchComplainerMakeYourVoiceHeardAttend

I trust my doctors and believe they're committed to my health but I depend on Jesus. He is my strength and redeemer. #HealingHandsOfJesus

Excuses are destructive, as they eliminate the possibility of fault and execute a litany of blame with no desire to change. #NoMoreExcuses

Some people have no desire to compete with excellence, as they know it's a losing battle. They prefer to try to eliminate it. #Encroachment

Nowhere in the Bible does it indicate that the world controls your happiness or rations your joy, but surrendering control creates regrets.

You think they don't understand. They clearly get exactly what you're trying to convey, but refuse to comply by disregarding your needs.

When you have a relationship with Christ, you refuse to allow doubt or fear to dominate your perspective. He has total control. #TrustHim

When God is the source of your strength, shocking news is really no different than any other information you receive. #ReactRespondRelease

Success isn't a surrogate for failure or mediocrity. If you desire nothing or are content with being average then success won't carry you.

Success doesn't partner with those who have an anchor on their ankle, despite their attempt to make you stay. #MovingForwardWithoutYou

It can be frustrating to be stuck on the runway but God is in total control of your final destination. Just be patient. #BlessingOnTheRunway

Unlike an aircraft, having your life on autopilot has many inherent dangers. We must continually strive to become better. #SoarToNewHeights

We face trials daily and some are certainly more challenging than others, but in our resolve we find courage and strength. #ReadyForToday

Successful people are least concerned with irresponsible people, as they know their efforts only produce poor outcomes. #WitnessTheFailure

My Tweets to You

Sometimes life will push you to the edge as you stand on a block of ice. But just hold on. He's sending an angel. #EdgeOfDestiny

Imagine the impact it would create if the world was without electricity. We would have to make the most of the sunlight. #MaximizeYourDay

What incites your hunger? What intensifies your thirst? I was starving for knowledge and had a thirst for truth. I discovered Jesus. #ImFull

If you had to choose one word to describe yourself, what would it be? Although we're more dynamic than one word, mine is love. #ForGodIsLove

Allow your struggle to birth your success. In the midst of battle, I began to think beyond my situation & my dream was born. #JoyInStruggle

The advancement of modern medicine has undoubtedly improved life expectancy, but only God can provide immortality. #TheEternityOfHeaven

Jesus went into places of affliction, pain and sin, not to harbor judgment and contempt, but solely to introduce love. #EndlessLoveOfGod

Social media outlets have provided a platform for the voiceless & vocal. But for some it has become a virtual bully arena. #DestructivePosts

What would you be willing to give up in exchange for something you desire? You can't gain abundance by being uncertain. #GiveUpDoubtBelieve

To foolishly seek the approval and validation of others is to run the risk of losing the greatest and most loyal supporter. #EndorsedByGod

Once Adam and Eve ate from the forbidden tree, they hid and covered themselves. How do you respond to hearing the truth? #CoveringNakedTruth

Some people desire to be seen and heard. Some desire to be loved and remembered. Some are content with being forgotten. #HeartOfDesires.

Having insurance provides a sense of protection. But God's protection is unparalleled, and Jesus already paid the deductible. #InsuredByGod

Uniforms can indicate your profession but not necessarily your character, as that is largely based on your disposition. #TemperamentOfChrist

Low self-esteem is one of the biggest killers of potential for it restricts your ability to dream. Confidence opens the door of opportunity.

A daughter should first learn of her beauty through the eyes of her father, which builds her confidence. You're pretty! #IKnowMyFatherToldMe

Ad hominem means rejecting an argument as a fallacy based on an irrelevant fact, like Jesus is only a carpenter's son. #TheFallacyOfNazareth

No amount of logic is sufficient for someone who's committed to not listening. Wisdom understands common sense can be uncommon. #StopTalking

My Tweets to You

What's your standard? What's your outlook? What's your expectation? Higher standards produce a better outlook and greater expectations.

As a child, you want freedom but it comes with a price of responsibility, and because your parents love you, they don't give it prematurely.

I will always be an agitator for truth, the person who frequently rocks the boat. I know how to swim and if I should drown #GodWillSaveMe

If someone gives you power, please understand they have the power to take it away. My strength comes from the Lord. #YouHaveNoPowerOverMe

People will build an army to fight truth. But regardless of the number of people who've assembled, their efforts are defeated. #TruthWins

Two types of people fight the truth: those who refuse to change and those who will continue to lie. #WhyAreYouFighting

Moving on is normal but staying where you are dissatisfied is completely abnormal. Stop rationalizing your behavior. #JustMoveOn

Who can love the unlovable, give to the ungrateful, forgive the unforgivable, kiss the undeserving & die for the unbeliever? #HisNameIsJesus

Fear can be relentless and continues to knock at your door but beyond the annoyance, your faith never allows you to answer. #NotHereForFear

The depth of the ocean & the endless trees in the forest represent the captivating presence of nature. #NatureIsGodsCreativity #SeeTheBeauty

Spring indicates change and growth, whether it be cleaning or gardening. However, you must work to achieve results. #SpringToWork

When you have a relationship with Christ, you live life as if you're in a room without a ceiling, knowing that possibilities are endless.

You can choose the Son & experience the beauty of His sunset or you can choose your own path & feel the heat of wrath. #SonOfGodShineOnMe

The biggest problem that people lacking drive typically have with a highly successful person is their courage to be extraordinary.

Fear has tunnel vision and only sees what lies ahead or within the line of vision, but faith sees the seemingly intangible and invisible.

Success creates problems that test your leadership. If you desire to overcome them, you must be willing to make tough decisions. #IDecided

Leaders respond to problems not by avoiding conflict but by being flexible in their approach & determined to find solutions. #ProblemsToFix

Some people think they need it all and will do anything to obtain it, but they must understand greed leaves you empty. #GreedASilentKiller

My Tweets to You

We might forget someone's name or even their face, but we rarely forget how we were treated. We remember love and pain. #IRememberYou

You can quickly tell if someone loves their car—it shines inside & out. But it takes work. Our relationships are no different. #LoveTuneUp

What do you want others to remember about you? Humor, loyalty, strength, success? I prefer they remember my love for Jesus. #RememberHim

You can visit the Sistine Chapel and marvel at paintings that adorn the walls, but nothing is greater than God's creation of you. #MadeByGod

We all have routines, whether it's morning breakfast or reading the local newspaper. In our routines we find our purpose. #RoutineSuccess

Clearly the speck in my eye captivates your focus.
But you blatantly disregard the plank in your own.
#TakeALookAtYourselfStopStaringAtMe

Despite your intellectual brilliance or financial prowess, your health must be a priority. Your body is a temple. #HealthyLiving

Leaders understand how to provide & receive direction. Followers just follow. Without being arrogant, learn to follow your own lead. #Leader

If you're hoping for me not to finish, you're certainly wasting your time. My aspirations aren't inspired by me but by God. #WatchUsFinish

It's important to set goals but you must be just as motivated to see them to completion by doing the necessary work. #GoalAccomplished

Movie producers, political candidates & persons of success quickly learn they can't please everyone, nor do they try. #PleaseFansNotCritics

Some people believe entrepreneurship is for those individuals who can't handle the demands of corporations, but that's untrue. #UncagedBird

Some people are willing to try anything except what they know is right. But their rebellion against truth only has one victim—themselves.

How you treat others is an indication of the longevity & fulfillment you'll receive from your success. #AllowYourSuccessToRepresentKindness

The concept of love shouldn't only be tied to the tangible. People and things offer inherent disappointments, but God's love is unwavering.

Complaining can certainly draw a large crowd but those who stand on the outskirts of this reality are busy searching for solutions. #TryIt

Love should be given without expectation or hesitation, but trust is earned. A wise person knows trust can be compromised by man. #TrustGod

We close our windows and lock our doors, as it adds a perceived level of protection, but why aren't we as cautious with our hearts? #Guarded

My Tweets to You

As a child, your imagination is limitless, your energy is relentless & your potential is endless. Don't allow anyone to impede your destiny.

My dreams surpass your imagination. My creative genius is greater than your exploration. My favor is inconceivable. #ImAChildOfGod

The Titanic was said to be unsinkable. Dictators deem themselves invincible. Scientists explore the unimaginable. #GodCanDoTheImpossible

A jewelry thief doesn't rob an empty store, nor does an art enthusiast marvel over a poorly painted replica. #YourEnemyKnowsYourValue

When my strength weakens, I depend on God .When friends are few, I depend on God. When man tells me no, I depend on God. #AlwaysDependOnGod

You can't want more & do less. You can't succeed by cutting corners. You can't win with a bad attitude. Don't be average. #BeExtraordinary

If anyone attempts to make you believe wanting the best is not desirable or realistic, then chances are they like being average. #WantMore

Several factors are used to rate restaurants, and while quality, presentation, taste and ambiance are important, service is key. #5Star

Resumes, cover letters and interviews are based on communication and writing skills. Great companies only hire the best. #EnhanceYourSkills

Email and social media have drastically improved the speed of communication and the sharing of information, but we must respond. #InboxFull

We've traveled for a long time, but because I love myself too much I can't continue on a road to nowhere. #DivergentPaths #TravelToPurpose

Forgiveness is all I know. It represents freedom from resentment and festering pain. I refuse to allow bitterness to resonate. #IForgiveYou

It's difficult to require someone to treat you with the highest level of respect when you boldly represent disrespect. #DoubleStandard

Creativity is a gift, while plagiarism is stealing someone else's work as your own without acknowledgment of the originator. #RetweetPlease

They smile in your face, laugh at your jokes, comfort you in sorrow and celebrate in your victory, but it's not genuine. #EnemyInDisguise

I smile when my heart's heavy, give when my resources are few, love when it hurts, listen when I'm tired, forgive when asked. #IAmAFriend

The record player, 8-track, cassette tape, CD and MP3 player exemplify the progression of technology. We must advance. #HowHaveYouProgressed

I see you watching and frequently respond to your inquiries, but neither my answers nor your awe replace the fact you need to focus on you.

My Tweets to You

It's easy to say you're working hard to complete your goals,
but at some point talking needs to translate into real work.
#GoBeyondTalk

Life can present itself as a puzzle & if you're not careful, you'll become frustrated trying to finish it by yourself.
#GodHasMissingPieces

Outside of God, it's tough to ask others to accept and love you
when you struggle to love yourself. You are more than enough.
#LovingMeFirst

The melting point of gold is 1,948 degrees Fahrenheit.
It seems to take intense heat to form value and purpose.
#AllowGodToIncreaseTheHeat

Frustration clouds your judgment by introducing doubt into your
mental state but perseverance breaks down the wall of doubt.
#DontQuitNow

Winners who operate with a high level of integrity, confidence
& humility don't arrogantly brag about their accomplishments.
#NoiseOfLosers

When you're waiting for your dream to materialize and it
seems your wait has been extended you might begin to doubt.
#TrustHimWaitAndBelieve

The enemy speaks your language and appears to be a
trusted friend but wisdom allows you to see their ways.
#SeeTheTricksAndRecognizeTheLies

It's not good to be insensitive, but you must not allow the problems of others to consume you. We all have problems to face.
#NotMyProblem

Please understand I don't think I'm better than anyone nor do I believe arrogance is admirable, but I make no apologies for my success.

A police officer enforces the law. A lawyer practices the law. A judge decides on the law. As citizens we follow the law. #LawAbidingCitizen

Although some mornings you feel imprisoned by the comfort of bed, you realize you can't achieve success lying down. #AwakeReadyForSuccess

Favor is not based on talent or ambition. It's God's grace. While I might not seem qualified in your eyes, God has positioned me at the top.

The saying misery loves company is unfortunately true, as those who are unhappy surround themselves with similar people. #LeaveMiseryAlone

Buried resentment or even justifiable blame are no excuse for retaliation, unforgiveness or hatred. The best relief for hurt is love. #TryIt

We all have gifts. That's God's promise to humanity. But what we choose to do with them is an individualized concept. #UnwrapYourGifts

Some marvel at your commitment & tenacity. But instead of being captivated by someone else, perhaps they should develop their own talents.

In schools, students are assessed using tests. Employers use performance appraisals. But self-assessment is just as important.

My Tweets to You

A person with a can-do attitude sees the inherent challenges and recognizes their limited abilities, but presses forward anyhow. #IKnowICan

Whether you lose your hair, agility or mental sharpness, you experience some level of decline as you age. But love grows. #Ageless

Don't define yourself by the expectations of others. Their inquisitiveness is not always out of concern or encouragement. #MyTimelineMyWay

The pressure will become intense but you must be unbreakable. God gave you a triple threat: talent, ambition and opportunity. #NeverGiveIn

People will always ask how you did it with no support, no money, and seemingly no hope. But you respond with, "Did you factor in God?"

Your wait has been intense & you've lost support along the way, but those who stood in loyalty & love will see your victory. #TooBadYouLeft

Some people are turned off by the competitive nature of others but in a world of limited resources, you must compete to win. #WinnersCompete

Success doesn't politely ask for your sacrifice. It demands it. If you think success is easy, you're mistaken. #SuccessRequiresSacrifice

People who truly need help are those who are least likely to ask. However pity or handouts is not what they desire. #SenseTheNeed

The saying nice people finish last is untrue. Kindness takes you further than evilness. Those who don't agree will watch you finish first.

There is no one pathway to success. Some use their athleticism, technical skill or ingenuity, but all paths require hard work. #IDidItMyWay

Although the popular group appears to be the best option, many times they miss opportunities because of shallow focus. #PopularityFades

Who will love you when you're old and gray or sit with you when you have little to say? Make an investment in love and it won't abandon you.

A time clock tracks the hours you work but is incapable of knowing your productivity. You can cheat an employer but not God. #HeSeesAll

Love can be fickle or sweet. Love can be verbal or nonverbal. Love can be loud or quiet. Love can be sensitive or tempered. #LoveCanBeYou

Adoration from your Father is a memory that lasts a lifetime, for it validates the unconditional love He has for you. #GodAdoresYou

You can spend all your time in a discovery phase, without making a concrete decision about your future. Stop procrastinating! #TimeToDecide

Your competition isn't those who are far behind but those who are running neck and neck. The race of success isn't won looking backwards.

My Tweets to You

Getting to the top doesn't mean you step on people to build your success but you can certainly step over those who desire nothing. #ExcuseMe

You can become tired from a night of partying, a long day of extended failure, or chasing your dreams. #WhichTiredAreYou

You can spend all your time convincing someone, or you can allow life to teach them a lesson greater than your words can convey. #YouWillSee

When you experience a muscle cramp, you don't hesitate to relieve the pain. Emotional pain must be met with the same resolve. #NoMorePain

My hard work isn't in response to someone's expectations nor is it intended to attract an audience. It represents my faith. #GodRewardsMyWork

You can make yourself believe you're not good enough. Conversely, you can make yourself believe you're the best. #ConfidenceIsMyOnlyBelief

Hatred can be powerful & sinister but love is a force which cannot be overpowered by hate. Love will always overshadow hatred. #LoveNotHate

People who are judgmental isolate people by using decisive tactics, but love is the best method of encouragement. #GodIsTheJudgeNotYou

Be a visionary. Be a person of integrity. Be wise in your decisions, proud of your accomplishments and humble in your victory. #BeTheBestYou

While you can't always win, you must not be content with second place. Being close to victory is not victory at all. #WinningIsStandard

It's imperative we serve others with no expectations. God instructs us to serve others with our time, talent & resources. #TheAbilityToServe

Vision relies on the intangible, believes in the seemingly impossible, and works tirelessly to become incomparable. #VisionOfGreatness

The narrow constraints of race and class distract us from the commonality of what we have termed humanity. #WeAreHuman #WeAreOne #WeAreLoved

Successful people are often criticized but despite this reality, they always think about the big picture. #SeeingBeyondCriticism #BigPicture

Some people are adamant that they know how to do something, despite never having done it. #FakeExpert

Your toughest opponent will never be your greatest challenge. The biggest challenge we all face is doubting ourselves. #NoMoreDoubtBelieve

If you're not wise, you'll spend most of your life searching for what you think you want only to discover your desires were misguided #Tired

Insecure people create tension between themselves & successful people as a means to avoid stepping out of their comfort zone. #BeABetterYou

A child develops in stages, from babbling to talking and from crawling to walking. We must constantly develop our minds & capacity to learn.

Those who complain & make excuses openly dismiss solutions & operate in a vacuum of negativity & blame, with no desire to change. #Solutions

The fable of the *Three Little Pigs* offers great insight as to how one must build a foundation stronger than your enemies'. #Indestructible

Although it seems impossible to encourage someone who's accepted defeat, you might be the angel God sends when they've given up. #YouCan

Having a strong faith gives you perspective and understanding to navigate life but without it, you're always left questioning. #FaithToStand

An attitude of defeat will produce defeat. Despite the intensity of your current situation, you must remain positive & hopeful. #GodWillDoIt

Can you handle rejection as gracefully as you do victory? "No" is heard by the greatest of people, but they aren't defined by it. #NoForNow

The causality of bad politics is that no one wins. Despite the stronghold of political parties, we're one nation under God. #LibertyForAll

Interrogate your relationships for purpose, truth and partnership. Many people fail because they refuse to see the obvious. #EnemyInDisguise

It's better to admit your wrongdoing than defend it. It's pointless to have a heated debate when you know your argument is based on lies.

We must not allow our privilege to restrict our compassion for others. On a global scale, fresh water is a privilege. #NotBlindedByPrivilege

What you possess pales in comparison to how you treat others. Unfortunately, wealth and kindness aren't synonymous. #WealthOfLove

The crucifixion of Jesus Christ teaches us that love is a demonstration. Thus love is more dynamic than words & promises. #TheActionsOfLove

U.S. currency boldly says IN GOD WE TRUST, but in some schools prayer is strictly prohibited & replaced by a moment of silence. #InGodIServe

Those who consider themselves knowledgeable know that knowledge isn't only intended for self, but is best when shared. #KnowledgeToShare

Granny's secret recipe has no value if she dies with it. Don't allow your talents to be imprisoned by your refusal to share. #TalentToShare

Having a great personality coupled with a great attitude makes your success more admirable. #WinningPersonality #GreatAttitude #Success

If you chase success with perseverance, passion & talent, chances are you'll catch it. But you must welcome the pursuit. #RunningAtFullSpeed

My Tweets to You

The ingenuity of Jobs. The financial genius of Buffet. The competitiveness of Jordan. The brilliance of Einstein. #GreatnessIsEarnedNotGiven

A missed opportunity is no opportunity at all. Those who want success seize every opportunity without hesitation. #MyApologiesYouAreTooLate

No matter how tarnished gold becomes, underneath is radiance, beauty & value. We have gold inside of us despite our flaws. #BelowTheSurface

It's one thing to be reflective & remember the past. But if you find yourself stuck in yesterday you most certainly will miss today. #MoveOn

In the corporate world, you understand that despite your talents, you are replaceable. But God knows you're irreplaceable. #OnlyOneYou

Some people only focus on your negative attributes which lacks encouragement but if they focused on the positive they would know your potential.

An entrepreneur doesn't have a boss to whom they must report, but a true business owner reports to themselves daily. #TheBossAndBottomLine

You can surround yourself with people who can help to inspire your dreams or those who will tear them down with negativity. #DreamBuilder

The competition is fierce but if your motivation to compete is nonexistent, you've already accepted defeat. #LoserByForfeit #GetInTheGame

Eugene L. Moore

LET THE TWEETS GO ON

The backyard was once a place of fun and creativity, but now our kids have their beats turned up and their minds tuned out. #TurnOffTheNoise

Parents, don't allow the television to become your child's baby-sitter, Play Station to become their friend and failure to be their reality.

Youngsters, there are 24 hrs in a day & you spend most of them sleep, on the phone, on social media & watching TV. #NonProductiveLessOptions

There's no get-rich-quick scheme or gimmick for success, nor is talent alone sufficient. You must put in the work. #ItTakesHardWorkPeople

Some people thrive on controversy and conflict and will do anything to create it. You must avoid such people at all cost. #HaveNoPartsOfIt

Untruths must be continually fed with more un-truths, but the truth is self-sufficient and unapologetic. #LivingOutsideTheTruthIsExhausting

The mind is extremely powerful and you can make yourself believe just about anything, but at some point lies concede to truth. #TruthWins

Many Americans aren't investing in their retirement, nor are they concerned with establishing a meaningful companionship. #LovelessPortfolio

You can't change the rules in the middle of the game. You must be practical in your approach and set standards at the onset. #RulesToFollow

You'll get tired, you'll contemplate quitting & you'll lose friends, but the reward is far greater than your sacrifice. #ThePriceOfSuccess

When you're in the presence of success the question shouldn't be what can you gain but what do you have to offer? #SuccessHasNoHandouts

People who have both success and wisdom do not randomly invite outsiders to their inner circle, but are more strategic. #AdmissionToSuccess

Those who experience success have made huge sacrifices, whether it is with their time or going against popularity. #SuccessAndSacrifice

Anger has the ability to minimize your character. Forgiveness has the potential to maximize it. We must be slow to anger. #Forgiveness

Relationships need many things to be successful, but without growth in your relationship, all other advances are marginal. #GrowthPotential

An elevator that doesn't rise is only a room with a door. Success is always taking you somewhere higher because of your motivation. #GoingUp

Who waters a dead plant? All the leaves have fallen and the roots have been over saturated. Don't continue to waste time! #WaterWhatGrows

A parasite is an organism that lives off another organism. People can behave as parasites and deplete your resources. #DontBeAHost

My Tweets to You

Be aware of professional takers. They typically present them-selves as loyal & trusted friends, but their primary role is to take. #FireThem

Some people approach you with an attitude of what can you do for me? But be wise enough to know your time & energy aren't for everyone.

Hypocrisy is real, for it allows you to easily see the flaws of others but fails to acknowledge your identical flaws. #FocusOnYouNotOnMe

Unfortunately, many children are emulating what they see in mu-sic videos but what they can't see is the green screen of illusion. #FakeVideo

Manufacturing jobs are obsolete & trade schools have lost popularity Youth must pay attention and aspire to attend college. #JoblessReality

If you stood behind the scenes of success, you would discover there's more to it than recognition. It entails many sleepless nights. #ImUp

You can wait on others to give you what you think you deserve or you can establish a reputation of excellence & name your price #TheyWillPay

Success is relative. While society might define it by per-sonal accolades, wealth or power, others might not agree. #DefineYourOwnSuccess

The essence of time escapes us. The mystery of the un-known intrigues us. The power of love captivates us. #LifeIsSoMuchBiggerThanUs

You can spend all your time chasing and settling for
pieces of love or you can wait for the whole experience.
#FragmentsOfLove #CompleteLove

To have a great day, you must have a great attitude. You can't
control what happens in a day but you can control your reaction
to it all.

Everyone will not be an academic. Everyone will not be a leader.
Everyone will not be rich. But no one can be a better you.
#YouAreAnOriginal

You can spend your time shunning those who are smart, accus-
ing them of arrogance or elitism, but where does that get you?
#LoveToLearn

Attempting to build a future with someone who pres-
ently isn't interested is a waste of valuable time.
#PresentEffortCanPredictFutureResults

Some people lose not because they lack intelligence but because
they lack initiative. It takes initiative to try and perseverance to
win.

Vision gives you hope. Indecision, confusion and passiv-
ity give you limited options and don't create a clear vision.
#HaveVisionHaveHope

Good teachers serve a vital part in developing our children but
it's ineffective without the support of parents & community
#ItTakesAVillage

Success has no room for the hopeless, no pity for excuses, no comfort for the weak and no patience for laziness.
#SuccessHasNoPrisoners

My Tweets to You

Life can throw curve balls and we miss many on our own,
but we must allow God to step to the plate and swing for us.
#HeAlwaysHitsAHomerun

Now that the finish line is within your sight, the enemy will start to work overtime but God will fire the enemy
#EnemyPinkSlip #MyPromotion

Things of great value require hard work to acquire. Present
yourself as someone who deserves the best and you'll attract it.
#KnowYourValue

You can create a scene by displaying poor behavior or you
can allow your positive presence to become the scene.
#SceneOfGreatnessSceneOfYou

Movies and life are comprised of many scenes and what makes
them most effective is the ability to play our part flawlessly.
#SceneOneAction

I've made mistakes. I've learned lessons. I've hurt others. I've
given love. I've chosen forgiveness. I've sought greatness.
#IHaveNoRegrets

Successful people focus largely on their key priorities and
spend minimal time focused on things of little or no value.
#ShiftYourFocus

You can allow man to be your center but will quickly
learn man is incapable of providing complete fulfillment.
#GodIsTheCenterOfMyAttention

If most of your time is spent analyzing the lives of others,
then clearly you haven't spent enough time analyzing yourself.
#SelfAnalysis

It's great to be a cheerleader or a supportive fan. But at what point will you discover you're greater than the sideline? #StepInTheGame

Don't hesitate to give. If all you had were two fish & five loaves, would you share? Giving shows God that you're thankful. #GiveMore

The prerequisite for failure is laziness & mediocrity, but for success it's hard work & excellence. What class will you take? #Excellence101

If you desire to be exceptional, you learn to make no exceptions for those who make excuses for their mediocrity. #IMadeItWithoutExcuses

We all desire to be happy but if we're searching for happiness in the wrong places with the wrong faces, you'll end up outside of happiness.

No one is going to execute your dream or vision better than you. But if you are waiting to be inspired by others, then you're wasting time.

It's unfortunate that some people are willing to listen to advice from their fake friends but rebel against those who truly love. #BadAdvice

God rewards effort with favor but He rarely gives victory to the effortless. Laziness doesn't create good outcomes. #ItTakesEffortToSucceed

Don't wait until you're old to realize the importance of time. Make the most of every second by aspiring to do your absolute best. #TimeToDo

For those who believe mistakes can magically correct themselves, you're sadly mistaken. Avoid making unnecessary mistakes. #NoUndoOption

For every expert there's a beginner. For every loser there's a winner. For every saint there's a sinner. #WeAllStartSomewhere #GreatEnding

As a child, blaming bad parents for your mistakes might be appealing. But as an adult, you must accept some responsibility. #OwnYourMistakes

Not everyone has an abundance of support from parents. Just ask an abandoned child. But you must develop inner strength. #SelfDetermination

As a young child, your parents would wake you up for school. But as you got older, you understood the value of an alarm clock. #TimeToGetUp

Words are powerful. People can say some hurtful things. But wisdom is far more powerful. Wise people know how to tune out negativity. #Muted

If you can't share your dreams with your friends because they're unsupportive & envious, then change your friends. #FriendsSupportEachOther

Goals are relative. As a teenager, you may want a driver's license. As a young adult, you may want to finish college. #AimHigherWorkHarder

Success might begin with a dream or vision, but it most certainly ends with continual hard work. You must make it happen! #DreamsIntoAction

If the view from your window was an alley, would you venture to say there's nothing to look at or there's nothing to see? #TakeACloserLook

You sent a friend request, asked to be followed, & gave an invitation, but your social media request has been denied. #TryGodHeAccepts

The power and the will to win are a powerful force but having no desire to win or being content with being average is powerless. #TryToWin

We've heard that bad habits are hard to break, but good habits are easy to form. Form a habit of kindness and love. #GoodHabits

If I fail, it was because I was told "no" or perhaps my timing was off. But no one will be able to say I failed because I didn't try.

There's no consensus on how to obtain success but the greatest commonality among successful people is perseverance. #HowLongWillYouWorkForIt

An excuse requires a conscious effort to exempt yourself from blame. We all make mistakes but not everyone makes excuses. #StopMakingExcuses

Excuses are convenient distractions created to disguise ones inability to accept responsibility for their lack of accountability. #NoExcuses

If you're searching for someone to motivate you to take the next big step toward your future, you're likely wasting your time. #SelfMotivated

My Tweets to You

Children have many influences, ranging from media to friends. But none should be more impactful than loving parents. #InfluentialParent

A true friend is rare, for they love when it's difficult, are loyal when others walk away and forgive even when it hurts. #MyOneTrueFriend

Legendary guitarist BB King coined the phrase The Thrill is Gone. Reconcile your relationships before it is too late. #LoveAndInterestsFade

Unlike the world, God gives us an opportunity to seek forgiveness without constantly reminding us of our mistakes. I am better than my past.

Attempting to avoid your problems by living in denial at some point will become too tiring. Get help from the problem solver! #FixItWithGod

Famous artwork like the Mona Lisa or documents like the Constitution have been preserved for centuries. Create things of value. #BeTimeless

We are destined to have some dark days but it's imperative we don't invite darkness into our lives and allow the enemy to exploit our pain.

If you're driving during a blizzard and notice several cars in a ditch, are you fearful or thankful? #YourPerspectiveMatters

The world builds your talent & inspires your greatness, but it can create conceit. Talent is man-driven but God-given. #BeHumbleOrBeHumbled

You can spend your entire life blinded by the frailties of life or you can accept that God's in control #NoLongerBlindedByLife #CanYouSeeNow

Why not me? When asked out of arrogance or envy it lacks decorum but for those who desire to be exceptional it's a great question. #WhyNotMe

No handouts were given, no special accommodations were made, nor was my talent exceptional. Just a strong work ethic! #GodRewardsDiligence

Youth need us to invest in their dreams and challenge them to reach beyond their potential. Encouragement goes a long way! #InvestorOfDreams

If you were unwilling to throw the ball in the backyard, then be unwilling to ask for sideline tickets to my pro game. #AttractedToMySuccess

We have become so hidden by our screens. A phone call has become a text. The family photo album has become a selfie. #AScreenshotOfEmotions

Although we live in a nation that celebrates individuality and competitiveness, it's so much better when we operate as a team. #ThePowerOfWe

If you choose to live your life as if it's a rat race, chances are you'll never accomplish your goals. Change your approach! #StopChasingAir

At an early age children are introduced to the need for structure. As responsible adults, we should know its value. #TheStructureOfSuccess

If you focus all your attention on the future, you'll become blind to the present. Seize the present moment of opportunities. #SeeTheNowPlan

Motivation and expectation aren't the same. While you might be expected to win, you must be motivated. #MyMotivationExceedsYourExpectation

You can attempt to find a lazy billionaire or a mediocre winner but those who desire to be great are awake when you're asleep. #GetMoving

It's foolish to believe laziness leads to success. If you desire success then you must work hard even when you're tired #TheEffortsOfSuccess

Super Bowl Sunday showcases the collective talents of two teams who, despite being plagued with injuries, still compete. #PlayingInPain

If you fail in school, a makeup exam or grading on a curve can help. But in life, failure can have irreversible consequences. #GetTheLesson

The most expensive automobile must have a fuel source in order to be driven. As humans, we too must have a fueling source. #FueledByGod

The greatest gift is giving. The greatest emotion is love. The greatest challenge is forgiveness. The greatest creation is you. #TheGreatest

The cost of education is continually rising but the cost of not having an education is a cost you cannot afford. What price will you pay?

Even if you live 100 years, time is always escaping your grasp. Thus, it's imperative to not complain. Embrace life. #NoTimeToWaste

It's foolish to know the truth & not apply it to your life. An acknowledgment of truth doesn't equate to an inward application. #UnusedTruth

Often times we start things with great excitement but over time, we lose motivation. We must be committed to the finish. #FromStartToFinish

Some people live outside of truth by focusing on image instead of reality. The reality is that images can be altered. #ThinkBeyondImage

Yesterday, no matter how great or terrible, is over. Embrace today with excitement. It's full of new possibilities. #OpportunityOverload

If you are blessed with longevity, you understand God renews our strength daily. Learn to love every moment of your life. #AgelessMiracle

No longer am I saddened by your envy and hatred, for now I know God will use it for fuel. Your hatred has fueled my greatness. #YouFillMeUp

It's not wise to seek approval from man, but it's imperative to understand that God's love is sufficient. #ToManImNothingToGodImEverything

NFL offensive lineman Derrick Coleman is legally deaf but never gave up on his dream to play football. #DeafDefyingHero #SuperBowlXLVIII

My Tweets to You

No education, power or influence gives you enough insight to understand God. Man isn't greater than the Creator. #TheArroganceOfMan

It takes faith to stand strong & wait on what God has promised as the world attempts to push you to your boiling point. #IntensityOfWaiting

In competitive sports, the home team is supported by the crowd and the opponent is the enemy. Silence a hostile crowd by winning. #SoQuiet

It's hard to be a winner when you have a losing mentality. A true winner tunes out doubt, fear, cynicism and negativity. #ICantHearYou

Courage isn't what you display when everyone is watching but it's instinctive. 8-yr-old Tyler Doogan saves 6 from a fire. #PintSizeOfCourage

We can quickly become consumed with gossip or useless chatter, but at some point, you must decide to shift your attention inward and change.

We live in a time where what you say can become breaking news. Intentionality or remorse don't erase the harshness of words. #WarOfWords

Each year we observe the accomplishments and leadership of MLK. But he wanted us to remember that he tried to love somebody. #ObserveTheLove

No matter how difficult your situation, you can always give a smile, a kind gesture, a listening ear, or a compliment. #TheGiftOfYou

Be a deciding person and decide to trust God. He has a winning track record. Take a moment and reflect on His past victories. #TrustVerified

The choices you make can determine your future. It is imperative to choose wisely, for mistakes can be costly. #ADecidingLife

No one knows everything, but it is foolish to desire to know nothing. Stupidity lives outside of truth and knowledge. #DesireToKnowSomething

Don't confuse love with judgment. Those who judge are not concerned with your improvement. But love aims to make you better. #SeeTheLove

Those who don't desire to change refuse to listen to anything that exposes their poor behavior. #ToListenOrNotToListenThatIsTheQuestion

His dream sought unity, but at the time it was unprecedented and unpopular. His Sacrifice. His Courage. His Legacy. Martin Luther King Jr.

An Olympian exudes extreme levels of dedication, desire and determination. Their quest for Olympic Gold is a captivating force. #GoldStandard

The pursuit of perfection is unattainable but the ability to do your personal best is always possible. Are you willing to push your limits?

To fail doesn't make you a failure. But when you decide to give up and relinquish your desire to try, then you experience true failure.

My Tweets to You

Failure isn't disguised but openly exposes its consequences.
No trickery was used but you willingly accepted the invitation.
#SayNoToFailure

No longer shall I make excuses for your poor choices. If I'm not
good enough to listen to, surely I won't be good enough to bail
you out!

You can sit in the presence of great wisdom and teaching
but consumption without application is only entertainment.
#ThePracticalUseOfWisdom

Rebellion leads to destruction. But when you listen to wisdom, you eliminate unnecessary mistakes.
#RebellionHasConsequences #CanYouHandleIt

Windows allow you to see the chaos of the outside but mirrors
allow you to see the beauty of the inside. Choose the mirror!
#LookingAtMyself

Look in the mirror and make no comparisons but embrace the
beauty of God's creation. The heart needs no makeup or fame.
#RevealTheRealYou

Beware of those who pretend to be a friend. Some of the greatest falls from success have come from the betrayal of a friend.
#JudasAmongUs

If you desire to be exceptional, you must refuse to make excuses and spend the majority of your time executing your plan.
#NoTimeForExcuses

Defying the odds is remarkable but proving your critics
right is devastating. True winners always silence their critics.
#BetterThanYouThink

My commitment is strong. My struggle is intense. My sacrifice is real. My enemy is plotting. My God is planning.
#MyRewardIsPriceless

No matter how great your accomplishments you must always remain humble, as life can take an unexpected turn.
#TheTwistsAndTurnsOfLife

When you're in a blizzard, your vision is impaired. You are cold and your sense of direction is compromised. All you can rely on is God.

It's in our distractions that we lose our sense of direction. Your ability to remain focused will lead you to victory.
#FocusToTheFinish

Everything in the world is in a constant state of change but God's love never changes. His love remains the same.
#TryTheNeverChangingGod

I searched for friends & found no one. I searched for Jesus & found everything. Now I know the true meaning of friendship.
#FriendOfChrist

Clean running water, freedom of speech, access to education, and the ability to exercise your faith are things we must not take for granted.

Twitter allows only 140 characters, forcing you to be concise. Some of the most powerful statements aren't long.
#LessWordsCanHaveMoreImpact

The vacation was awesome but your return flight has been delayed. Your annoyance is intense as you desire to get back home.
#NoPlaceLikeHome

My Tweets to You

Basketball has 48 minutes in regulation, football and hockey have 60, and baseball has 9 innings. Use your time to play, perform and win.

The power of nature is intense. The water rises, the wind blows, the heat soars, the temperatures plummet, and the storms roar. #NatureVsMan

Communication can be a stumbling block in many relationships. Learn to have healthy conversations and not verbal assaults. #ProductiveTalk

Once you discover your thinking is incorrect, you have two options. You can make excuses for your logic or you can change. #NewWayOfThinking

The underdog is not only misunderstood but is often excluded from any hopes of success. God endorses the underdog! #GuessYouNeverSawMeComing

Step one: The goals have been spoken, the list has been written and placed on the vision board. Step two: What's next? #SeeYourVisionThrough

Sometimes we feel isolated and trapped in our pain but despite the uniqueness of the situation, it's only new to you. God heals your pain.

Look back to learn from your mistakes. Look forward to focus on what lies ahead. Look to the present and change. #DoItNow

Did it work before? Then why do the same thing again? Do not become a repeat offender of failure. #BreakTheCycleOfFailure #ChangeItUp

Most homes have closets but the size varies. Do not focus all your attention on the bigger closet but learn to make the most of your space.

You can spend a lot of time assessing the talents of others or you can interrogate your own ability and perfect your talent #ChangeYourFocus

Be less concerned with what others think, as getting an A+ in approval is meaningless when you are failing in your relationship with God.

Knowing the most doesn't mean you'll make good decisions. Sometimes those who seem to know the least make better decisions. #UseWhatYouKnow

Every year we make resolutions, and those aspirations quickly fade in the horizons. Most change is met with hesitation. #WhyWaitChangeToday

Compliance is based on one's ability to follow rules but compromise is the ability to come to a mutual agreement. #AgreeToCompromise

Your effort or lack thereof is an indication of your desire to change. Those who want to change spend less time talking and more time doing.

The spider anticipates attack and creates a web to trap his enemies. Ultimately, the prey devours his predator. #WebOfProtection

The Goliath Bird Eating Spider is an interesting species, as it feeds off a much larger enemy. God prepares your main course. #EnemyAppetite

My Tweets to You

What does December 26th mean to you? For retailers more sales. For consumers more debt. For Christians more love. #BornSonOfGod #OurSavoir

As a child, life is all fun and games. During your 20s, it's one big party. True adulthood yields great responsibility. #NoLongerAChild

The most special days of your life will only last 24hrs. Christmas, birthday, wedding, graduation are all just one day. #MakeEachDaySpecial

Behold a Savior has been born! The nicely wrapped presents will become crinkled and the gifts will be an afterthought but His love remains.

You saw your dream up close but couldn't seize it. But don't worry. God gives us a sneak peek to remind us He delivers. #HeSeesYouLooking

There's no point in attempting to become someone you're not, for it's an impossible task. You were born to become the greatest YOU possible.

Movies are great as they allow us to witness art in motion but the greatest production ever is the script of your life. #TheUntoldStoryOfYou

Money can't buy it, fame can't secure it, & royalty is not an heir of it. Happiness is an illusion for those who don't know Christ. #KnowHim

To be inoculated with the vaccine of denial is no cure for pain but only blurs your ability to see and deal with the truth. #StrandOfTruth

The moment you remove the disguise & accept your flaws, you can conquer your insecurities & find peace in your own skin. #UnveilTheRealYou

You should have been grateful for your success and rise to the top but you displayed such arrogance now look how far you've fallen. #SkyFall

Allow your enemies to become your inspiration. Use their negative energy to fuel your success. They too recognize your greatness. #FuelToWin

When you're in IT sometimes, you can't see IT and might wonder if God is even behind IT. Don't be distracted by obstacles. #SeeItToTheFinish

Your pain is real and hurts intensely, but don't surrender to it. Allow your pain to lead you to your destiny. #GodMovesYouFromPainToPurpose

Blamers don't discriminate. They believe others are responsible for their mistakes but foolishly disregard the contributions of self.

Living in a web of lies takes extreme effort and distorts your reality. Living in truth avoids the distortions of dishonesty. #LiveInTruth

Gloves come in a pair, and when you lose one, you discover the importance of two. Hold on to those things that matter. #TwoPerfectGloves

Chasing your dream indicates your pursuit to find what God has promised. Don't fail to search and recover the blessings of God. #DreamFinder

My Tweets to You

You must be confident in your decisions because if you aren't, you will be forced to live with the consequences. #BadDecisionsDeepRegrets

Learn to live on a budget and do not attempt to live in the financial fast lane. The heavy traffic causes crashes. #StayInYourFinancialLane

People often say I'm trying, and in most cases, trying can be sufficient. But there are times when you must go above trying. #TryToJustDoIt

Success is a lot about organization. If you fail to organize, you will spend a majority of your time trying to get order. #TheOrderOfSuccess

You can easily expose all that I'm not but you're simply unwilling to admit all that I am. I am more than my flaws & your criticisms. #IAmMe

How someone treats you is an indication of what they think of you. More importantly, it shows how you think of yourself. #ImBetterThanThat

Mandela was a true champion of change. His relentless effort to fight against injustice changed a nation. What will be your legacy? #Mandela

Celebrating a milestone is a great moment of reflection and you should enjoy it. But what happens when the cheers have subsided? #WhatsNext

Can you see the finish line? Victory is within reach & despite your weariness, you must continue to push harder. #QuittingIsNotAnOption #Win

You have an education but no job. You have talents but no opportunity. You have wealth but no peace. God is the answer. #LifeHasNoGuarantees

You can continue to sit in an office with hopes of a brighter tomorrow or you can begin to chase your dreams today. #MakeAnInvestmentInYou

Computers and cellular phones use to be bulky and heavy 20 years ago, but now we have a variety of sleek and modern designs. #ChangeIsGood

My trial is my treasure, for it allowed me to dig deep into my soul and discover I could do all things through God. #IFoundHisTreasureChest

I'm quiet for a reason, so don't be nervous by the awkwardness of my silence. Soon you'll hear the noise of my success. #YourEarsAreRinging

You must be humble to accept advice but wise enough to know not all advice is rooted in sound judgment. I heard you but humbly disagree.

There's no magic formula or pathway for success but there are key principles to follow. Dream Big. Work Hard. Sustain It. #KeysToSuccess

There is no point in convincing others to believe in your dreams. You must believe in yourself. The enemy detours your dreams with doubt.

We attempt to manipulate time by changing our clocks, but if all the clocks stop, time continues to move. #DontLoseTrackOfTime #TickTock

My Tweets to You

Your test! Your trial! Your storm! We are willing to bypass our valley experiences but we must embrace the challenges of life. #YourVictory

Thank God for your trials for they represent your ability to stand in pain. Soon He will allow you to stand strong and tall. #JustStand

How do you transition from your trial to victory without having resentment towards those who celebrated your suffering? #WitnessHisWrath

Life's moving at lightning speed and failure to pay attention to its movement will force you to revisit moments of your past. #TodayIsTheDay

As a child learns to ride a bicycle, they often fall. Despite the tears and disappointment, they typically don't give up. #TryUntilYouGetIt

Some decisions are more complicated than a simple coin toss and you must be willing to approach them with patience #NoRush #TakeTimeToDecide

The right thing to do is often the hardest thing to do. Failure to do what's right and difficult can lead to deep regrets.

God knows the future but you struggle to accept the present and spend too much time focused on the past. #GiveHimControl #HeKnowsWhatsToCome

If you interview someone of greatness, you'll discover they were challenged to take a different path but chose their dream. #DreamYourWay

Children live in the world of Me, My and Mine. But if you grow in wisdom and love, you're concerned with Them, They and Those. #PowerInUs

The waiting game is not intended for non-dreamers but is reserved for those who can endure some of life's greatest hurdles. #ItsWorthTheWait

Preparation, Position and Perseverance are essential to success. Are you prepared? Have you positioned yourself? Do you have tenacity?

It's imperative not to seek financial success as a means to acquire happiness. The two are often mutually exclusive. #HappinessBeforeSuccess

We live in a society of consumerism and materialism. We are encouraged to purchase and we place value in having it all. #WhenIsEnoughEnough

Learning to walk away from toxic situations where you're emotionally connected is difficult but you're cursed if you stay. #BlessedInLeaving

The enemy attempted to kill you in the ocean's deep water but failed. Don't struggle to survive on the shallow shore. #ShallowWaterDeepFaith

Although you hurt me, I've reconciled my pain and have truly forgiven you, as I realize God allowed it all. #PromotionThroughReconciliation

You can choose to stay in the crowd to seek popularity and minimize your talent or be exceptional and create a crowd. #JoinMeOutsideTheBox

My Tweets to You

My profit for your success is zero. My advice is given as a courtesy. Your failure to listen to wisdom will cost you deeply #ThePriceOfPride

Whether you are an entry-level employee or an executive, your title or education doesn't determine your character. #TitleRichCharacterPoor

The New Year is always approaching but as the time nears, we make resolutions. But why wait to become better? #ChangeToday

A desk is typically a wooden structure used for various tasks like writing or studying and creates a space for work. #ADeskOfAccomplishments

Christians should never see eye-to-eye with a negative person. They have a deficit mentality, which contradicts your life. #PositiveOutlook

Having no complaints isn't an indication that you're free from issues but you realize complaining doesn't help the situation. #IWontComplain

The guests have departed and the table has been cleared. It's in the quiet moments that you can be reflective and thankful. #TimeToReflect

Never allow your situation or limitations to determine your expectation. God will bless you in spite of your weaknesses. #CanYouTrustHim

Fear stands still. Success keeps moving with expectation. Don't become paralyzed by fear. If you desire greatness, you must move. #RunForIt

At times, it seems the enemy has a slight edge. However, He rains on the just & unjust. In the end, you always pull ahead. #WinnerByLandside

So you did nothing? Failure to accept accountability creates issues like blame, excuses & an unwillingness to change. #IPlayedAPart

True friends applaud your success and minimize your failure with encouragement. Enemies only applaud your failure. #TheEnemyIsNoFriendOfMine

We must stop waiting for major holidays to express love, compassion and kindness, but must demonstrate our willingness to love daily.

Man manipulates our emotions by making us believe our life is controlled by an evil puppet master but God has total control of the strings.

Clouds obscure visibility and prevent you from seeing your destiny. When you travel with God, you have extreme clarity. #ClearSkiesToLand

You have so many questions and at times your frustration is intense, as you simply have no answers. Why me? Why now? What's next? #HeAnswers

In life, we have a beginning & an end, but our legacy is based on what we do in the middle. Maximize the moment. Don't waste time. #LiveLife

There is purpose in God's process. Even in the most tragic circumstances, God has a plan, although pain makes it difficult to see. #HoldOn

My Tweets to You

When you have limited options or have exhausted them all you must totally depend on God. In the future don't waste time. #TryGodFirst

Allow God to change you. The results will be pleasing. But when you change for the wrong person, you won't even recognize yourself. #WhoAmI

God has no intention of giving you a bootlegged copy, but if you are patient, you can experience the flawless original. #TheCopyrightsOfGod

A very wet paper bag symbolizes our capacity to carry burdens. Take your burdens to Jesus. At most, you can only carry a cotton ball.

A triangle is purposeful but can't fit into a circle of a smaller size without being altered. To force things to work causes pain. #NotAFit

Two are typically better than one unless someone represents a negative. Learn to seek relationships with growth potential #SeePositiveGrowth

Jailing a king doesn't mean they aren't free. Refuse to be a prisoner of pain. Ascend to greatness like Mandela, MLK and Jesus.

Don't give out of obligation or to be noticed, but from the heart with love. The recipient senses your intentions. #GivingWithoutExpectation

The pitcher of God's love is so great He can pour out a blessing you can't contain. But you must have faith. #FloodedWithBlessings

Whatever issues you face today, you don't have to face them alone. Bring the undefeated champion in the ring of life. #VictoryIsMine

Watching sports creates a wide range of emotions but the lesson learned is that no matter the outcome, the focus is always on the next game.

If you desire to spark the inquisitive nature of others, you must allow your actions to speak louder than your words #WhySayItJustDoIt

If you're in the dark and the lights come on, your eyes must adjust to the light. Don't be surprised how people look at you. #LightsOnBright

We must find a level of contentment in our uncertainty. It allows God to bring clarity. He knows, even when we don't understand. #LetHimDoIt

Memories of love echo into the future. Neither death nor calamity can stop the power of love for it transforms all situations. #EndlessLove

We can become reckless with our freedom to choose but we must be careful to account for the consequences of our decisions. #CanYouLiveWithIt

Be equally thankful for your failure and success. A lack of appreciation forces God to humble you by withholding his grace. #BeThankfulToGod

It's important to be pragmatic in making decisions, but don't go against your inner voice, as you'll have regrets. #TheVoiceOfGodNeverFails

They screamed for His crucifixion but were frightened by His death and silenced by His resurrection. #TheEnemyTriedToKillMeButGuessWhoIsBack

More than fifty years ago an assassin's bullet killed JFK and the nation was in disbelief. Those with great potential pose the greatest threat.

It's better to die on the verge of doing something great than to live and do nothing. JFK, MLK and a carpenter named Jesus.

We must be disciplined in our light & love, for failure to do so creates darkness birthed in pain. Hatred has no restraints. #TheLightOfLove

A lack of wisdom & restraint causes some to seek things, which have no true value or purpose. Be wise in your decisions and seek greatness.

Although my sacrifice has been great, it has tangible results. Things of great value require extreme effort & sacrifice. #SeeingMySacrifice

Life has many obstacles but those who overcome understand the importance of fighting frustration, fear, doubt & excuses #WhereIsTheFightInYou

You invited all your friends to the infancy stage of your dream but only a few attended. Now the dream is real and they all want in. #TooLate

Allow leaders to lead by not being cynical. Sometimes the best decisions are initially unpopular. Consensus is relative. #LeadershipToDecide

It's better to be exhausted from doing something of purpose than to be in a constant state of boredom from doing nothing #BeBoredWithBoredom

If you find yourself consumed with the business of others, you'll fail at life's greatest task of self-reflection. #FocusOnTheBusinessOfYou

If your presence incites the curiosity of others, then you are living with purpose. Greatness always becomes a spectacle. #VisibleGreatness

If you want God to make an investment in your dreams, do not become someone who falls at the moment of pressure. #ShowGodYouCanSoHeCan

Carry yourself in such a way that others are assured of your potential. If you want to become president then be presidential. #BeItToday

Preparation is an essential step of success. Broadway productions are based on countless hours of practice & refinement. #PreparationMatters

Unfortunately, we forfeit our destiny when we decide to covet the talents of others. Learn to maximize your talents and unlock your future.

It becomes critical for you to develop a specific goal or target, as moving aimlessly in life invites disappointment. #TheTargetOfSuccess

I sought your counsel but you either refused to help or offered little advice. Your denial forced me to rely on God. Thanks for not helping!

Don't allow the negativity of others to challenge your aspirations. With God, you're capable of doing things others cannot. #DoingItWithGod

Impatience leads to irrationality, which leads to a desire to manipulate your situation. Doing it your way voids God's efforts. #Wait

You can attempt to gain consensus for your lack of effort but ultimately you'll have to deal with the errors of your decisions. #NoExcuses

Persuasive tactics can influence behavior. Don't allow the persuasion of fear to impede your success by becoming your greatest critic.

If you're broken, you must be careful not to partner with someone who serves as your demolition. Broken can't fix broken. #LetUsBuildTogether

Those who invested in gold before it was a hot commodity are the greatest winners. The biggest losers are those who waited for popularity.

When you allow bitterness to take root in your heart, you destroy the growth that God has for you. Fill your heart with gladness. #JoyInside

If you're tired of waiting then the best alternative is to continue to wait with greater intensity. Impatience kills dreams. #WillingToWait

In my pain is where you will find my greatest strength. God orchestrated my fall so my enemies could witness my rise. #ImBetterThanBefore

How many times have you left the stands thinking your team lost, only to discover they won? Confidence never abandons victory. #StayToTheEnd

We must not become spoiled by our relationship with Christ. Just like our earthly parents, we can't always get our way. #LoveHisNoAndHisYes

Fear causes one to choke when an opportunity arises. In reality, the only threat to your success is your lack of confidence. #BreatheToWin

A winner is always focused on the next hurdle of success. Repeat 3-Peat! Learn to push your success to higher limits. #TheDemandsOfSuccess

Most people remember their youth, pain and love, but our lives become misguided when we live in the past. Take hold of your future. #SeizeIt

Have no qualms about getting older as the alternative is to live on the memories of the past at the expense of not enjoying the present.

If you fail to pay attention, you'll wake up one day and realize you're past your prime. Don't look back. Make the best of what lies ahead.

Foolish ambition is like a human chasing a cheetah. While your effort might be great, the outcome won't be favorable. #AmbitionToLose

Everything around us is moving: the light, traffic, animals the wind, the water and the waves, but you're standing still. #MovePeopleMove

My Tweets to You

Your enemy sees your potential and relentlessly attacks
but because of God's grace and mercy they never succeed
#EyewitnessToHisFailedAttack

I have learned to tolerate your selfishness & even your jealousy,
for I know my future doesn't include you. God's moving me
ahead. #StayBack

Never question your ability to give, for it indicates you're
in possession of resources that other people don't have.
#GiveAsItHasBeenGiven

A mother waits for a child to be born, a child waits to become an
adult. Life is filled with constant waiting. Wait patiently. #WaitOn

A sinkhole is a massive hole caused by a collapse in the surface
layer. Our problems can seem just as massive, but God is bigger.
#TryGod

Waiting for Godot-A Tragicomedy features two characters that wait
endlessly for a friend. In life, tragedy occurs when we give up
prematurely.

You are trying to convince God to move forward with your
approach, but He is simply saying He doesn't need your help.
#OnlyHisWayWorks

Our lives are built on the shoulders of our ancestors. A pecan
tree can live 300 years. Our ancestors planted for the future.
#AYieldingLife

Our story is unique, as it represents our journey. But the moment
we allow circumstances to dictate our destiny, we stop God from
writing.

As Christians, we maneuver through life knowing we are destined to have setbacks. We are often shaken but never broken. #ForGodRollsWithUs

A man claimed to be homeless and hungry but happy. Happiness is greater than your residence or appetite. Allow God to feed you. #FullWithGod

As the holidays quickly approach, many of us shift from contentment to excitement. Learn to live each day as a gift. #UnwrapYourJoy

The enemy has thrown his best punch & you feel the strength of his efforts. But as you are knocked down, you realize he has no power. #GetUp

We are hesitant to question success, but quickly question adversity. Successful people expect and plan for adversity without complaining.

To assess one's understanding, we often use tests as a measurement. God uses the instrument of trials to test our faith. #CanYouPassTheTest

If you hope success eliminates the bumps & bruises of life, you're sadly mistaken. Life happens irrespective of your success. #BraceYourself

Who among us is perfect? We all have flaws, but what makes us different is how we choose to deal with our imperfection. #ALifeOfFlaws

Opportunity can give you a head start but you must run with it, as failure to do so allows others to pass you by. Take the baton #RunForIt

Retailers create a false sense of reality, as the aisles of opportunity seem limitless. But if you're not careful, your shelf will be empty.

As a child, we're told to behave. As adults, we know poor behavior leads to bad decisions. Don't allow your behavior to get you in trouble.

Having designer clothes and no money is foolish. Seek the intangible nature of confidence. Don't charge success and bankrupt your dreams.

We wear it, we drive it, we want it, but do we truly have it? A part of SUCCESS is what you see, but the majority of it is in what you do.

Things of great value like health, joy, peace, family, friends, and love aren't worn but represent internal happiness. #EmptyHeartFullCloset

Wind thrusting across the ocean's water; rain falling upon the world's rooftops; snow blanketing the mountains. #SeeNaturesBeauty

Things that require a great deal of effort & talent are only attempted by a few. The greatest tragedy occurs when you fail to try. #TryToWin

Your success will cause some people to feel obligated to explain or justify their failure. Make no apologies for your success. #FailureTalks

Your courage, strength & sacrifice sway in the wind as the flag. Veterans, stand tall. Thanks for your service & commitment. #HonorAmongUs

Wounds must be treated, as they cannot withstand the pain. But scars must be revealed, for they represent your survival. #TestimonyOfScars

Be encouraged by those who are jealous, for there's something inside of you so powerful that it incites their jealousy. #GreatnessInsideYou

A toxic environment can cause the greatest believer to stumble. We must learn to love from a distance. Failure to do so causes our demise.

Often what we can't tolerate is what we're challenged to correct. If you hate lies then represent truth. Your passion leads to your purpose.

You are more than your name, as you're uniquely and wonderfully made. Your talent is sufficient and no one can be you or receive your gifts.

Success refuses to extrapolate its ideologies from fear or negativity. You must enter the game expecting victory. #BeCourageouslyPositive

Fear is contagious. If you are not careful, you will allow others to impede your plans by casting doubt on your vision. #GreatnessHasNoFear

You have plans but lack the resources for implementation. If God imparted the plans into your mind, be assured construction is inevitable.

When you build something of consequence or greatness, you must have a strategy. Without planning, you labor in vain. #BlueprintOfDestiny

My Tweets to You

We can spend all our time trying to figure out how our dreams will materialize but we are limited and must allow God to finance our vision.

The enemy has issued a warrant for your arrest, for he knows & fears what you'll become. Your potential is under attack. #OnlySurrenderToGod

A father is in the store and their child asks for a toy, but he fails to oblige because he knows wants from needs. #FatherGodKnowsBest

A family was stranded in a snowstorm for hours and began to lose hope but they were saved by a stranger on a snowmobile. #HoldOnHelpIsComing

Today could be the day for your breakthrough but you must get up with excitement and expectation, not sadness and doubt #AwakeWithExpectancy

Many of us have a need for speed but there is a greater need for us to slow down. Cherish each moment of the ride of life. #NoNeedToSpeed

Unlike man, God has no desire to pacify us but wants to bless us beyond measure. Don't allow the world to calm your purpose. #CryDestiny

A refinery takes raw materials and turns them into things of value like gold. If we endure God's process, our value increases. #HeRefinesYou

Whatever holds you captive causes your defeat. Is it insecurity, pain, blame, doubt, unforgiveness, or a lack of motivation? #BreakFreeWin

Being selfish is like a building without a foundation. Eventually the building collapses. A foundation of selfishness is unstable! #GiveMore

All you have is your FAITH. The world laughs at your dreams but God has planted a vision in your soul. Soon the doubtful will be humbled.

Sometimes the pain of your present situation makes you revisit your past. Remember. Reflect. React. He's done it before. #HeWillDoItAgain

There are four seasons of nature, which require us to change. Most of us wouldn't wear a winter coat in the summer. #DoNotResistChange

The valley prepares you for the mountaintop. But be advised: the enemy knows your potential and will attack. Are you ready? #LookToTheHills

My pain is strong; my God is stronger. My weeping is deep; my laughter is deeper. My flaws are wide; my strengths are wider. #ILoveMe

The valley experience should be your greatest memory. It demonstrates God's ability to stand with you in times of crisis. #HeWillRescueYou

Danger is real & is based on facts, e.g. a high voltage power line is dangerous. But fear is not real, as it manipulates the facts. #FearNot

Living a life not anchored in God creates a much turbulence. In life, we are promised pain. Can you handle the storm? #CheckYourAnchor

My Tweets to You

Great people are seekers of knowledge and truth. Ordinary people have a limited thirst for knowledge and often reject the truth. #BeGreat

We were once inseparable. But life happened and now our worlds are miles apart. Stop trying to bring outsiders to your destiny. #MoveOn

How do you find strength when the pain is unbearable? Your pain is beyond comprehension and you feel defeated. #HisResurrectionPower

The enemy attacks things we cherish—our health, family and finances. But his weapon is defective. #TheEnemyShootsBlanks

Favor is God's way of saying I'll give you abundance based on my grace not your merit. Your promotion isn't based on your skills. #HisFavor

God is calling but you send Him to voicemail. Stop rejecting His calls, for He knows all your faults yet loves & accepts you. #PleaseAnswer

It's through obedience that our blessings are birthed. Allow God to bless your obedience by providing a supernatural miracle. #MiraculousGod

You are praying but you hear nothing from God. It seems that His way is so hidden. Why is He not responding? Don't lose hope! #HiddenMiracle

When your needs are great, allow your dependence on God to be greater. Expect Him to answer. Nothing is too great for God. #HeCanDoAllThings

In order to receive an invoice that's paid by God, you must know that faith requires a work order. Do the work & He'll deliver. #PaidInFull

The enemy works on all sides but God works the middle. His ability to deliver despite the crisis that surrounds you is a miracle. #MiddleMan

The enemy attacks when the clouds are low. Don't be distracted by the storm, but press forward, as the sun is shining ahead. #IsolatedShower

Don't allow your detour to become your destiny. If you travel long enough on the wrong path eventually, you'll accept being lost. #WrongWay

It's game day! If you desire to win you must practice, perform and persevere. The fourth quarter is your moment for memories. #TimeToPerform

A distinct difference between mediocrity and greatness is that greatness never peaks prematurely but always soars higher. #RisingToTheTop

Pain doesn't stop laughter, but regret or blame can silence it. Learn to let things go! Move forward by not looking back. #LaughALittle

You can spend your life trying to be in the spotlight or you can accept that some of the greatest work is done behind the scenes. #LightsOut

Autumn is beautiful as the leaves display vibrant colors. We must embrace change, as the leaves of life are destined to fall. #AutumnBeauty

You can gather your thoughts before speaking or you can speak without thinking and discover you should have taken more time. #DoYouHearYou

Are you an extrovert or an introvert? Are your decisions based on thinking or feeling? We must be aware of our behavior. #PersonalityDefined

What drives you, God or greed? Greed is a continual need to acquire things but you're never satisfied. God is enough! #SatisfactionGuaranteed

Anger takes you to a place where you would love to forget but joy takes you to a place where you always hope to remember. #JoyInMemories

A lioness is methodical and doesn't chase every prey. Chasing and not catching or dying in the chase are not worth her effort. #ChasingSmart

The iteration "Live, Love, Laugh" seems so simple, but many use "Conform, Cry, Complain". Choose to live love and laugh. #ContagiousLaughter

Chasing every opportunity is not a strategic approach. Not every opportunity is worth your pursuit. #ThinkBeyondTheChase #MoveWithPrecision

Judging others gives the accuser a false sense of reality allowing them to ignore their mistakes. The judge becomes the accused. #JudgeNot

You paint a picture of happiness but as others look closely, they discover what you already knew—it was fake. #SeekGodNotTemporalHappiness

We will sit in the cold for a football game and stand for hours at a concert. But will we sacrifice our comfort for God? #ComfortInChrist

Humility is our ability to understand we are limited. Despite our talents and perceived greatness, we are nothing without God. #LimitedMe

Victory comes to those with great vision, for it's not easily distracted by the blurriness of life. Through God, we are always victorious!

There is no point in speaking darkness and doubt over your life, for you will force yourself to stumble. Allow the light to guide your path.

Learn to simplify your life, as it is not wise to complicate it. We are already promised pain. Why complicate things? #ASimpleLife

No two people have the same DNA or fingerprints. We represent the true nature of originality. It's impossible to be someone else. #BeOriginal

Life is full of ebbs and flows. Sometimes we are in disbelief over the way things turn out. Even in tragedy, God delivers. #TrialToTestimony

To love your enemies is challenging but some struggle to reciprocate love that's given. Don't allow pain to miscalculate the rarity of love.

Listening is a great attribute, but many of us struggle to listen to the right people. Who are you listening to? #EnemiesScreamGodWhispers

My Tweets to You

Liberation is freedom. Bondage is captivity. How much longer will you be held captive by the past? #WalkAway #DontLook-Back #FreedomLiesAhead

Ideally, a passenger's goal is a flight without turbulence, but your ultimate goal is to make it to your destination. #HisTurbulentBlessings

We represent the calming nature of the ocean's water but sometimes we get distracted by the waves. Learn to ride the waves. #ForwardThinking

You attempted to steal my peace but it is protected by Him. You asked if you can buy it but it's not for sale. #PeaceIsPriceless

Sleep is necessary, for it rejuvenates the body & allows you to function at your greatest capacity. Make a decision to be productive. #GetUp

Contentment is developed over time as it takes a great deal of trust. Ambition is great but at some point, we realize more is never enough.

In a real sense, you want something you have never had but you must do something you have never done. Don't be afraid to break the cycle.

What happens when your private sin becomes public? Things which are hidden in the shadows soon become center stage. #PrivateHasGoneViral

If you live a long life, you will acquire many things. But once you have it all, what more is there left to obtain? #SeekEternityNotThings

Your concern shouldn't be your reputation, for it's based on the opinion of others. But your integrity and character are based on you. #IAm.

The truth sometimes seems arrogant but this is a detour. The path of change begins when you accept truth without excuses #WalkInTruth

You can ascend to the top and have many friends but once you fall to your lowest and look around there is simply no one there. #WhereWereYou

The enemy whispers, "You have done enough. God has abandoned you. Please give up now." But God whispers, "Hold on my child." #ChooseHisVoice

We experience pain & disappointment which disrupt the flow of our lives, but we must allow God to carry our pain, for He has the capacity.

Pump up the volume! We can get lost in noise but what happens when there is silence can you accept your truth? You can't drown out truth.

There's no such thing as average greatness. If the people around you are uncomfortable with your success perhaps you're in an average crowd.

What do you see? What do you want? What have you done? What do you have? Success is about vision, desire, hard work & results. #BeStrategic

Someone who truly loves you toils all night while you peacefully sleep. Love's greatest concern is to eliminate worry. #LoveIs

My Tweets to You

Many people begrudgingly ask you how you're doing because they fear being placed in a position to help. Friends sense and supply the need.

You cannot continue to embrace temptation because at some point temptation wins. Playing dangerously leads to your defeat. #StopPlaying

Time is a fleeting resource. Please don't allow others to be reckless with your time, for it can never be replaced. #NoTimeToWaste

A distant, deferred, or delayed blessing is no indication that God won't answer your prayer, but you must exhibit faith. #HeFulfillsPromises

God provides a foundation for growth. If your life lacks growth, perhaps you haven't made space for God. Welcome Him inside. #HeBuilds

You can continue to contemplate what you need do and find yourself doing nothing, or you can decide to do something. #TalkersTalkDoersDo

We plant, water and wait, knowing only God can bring growth. When it seems like there are no signs of growth, we must trust Him. #GodCan

The sun sets and rises but how much longer will you allow time to pass you by? The only thing that isn't moving is you! #TimeMovesWithoutYou

God gave us mobility but we wanted more, so we created the automobile, train & plane. But no matter how fast you go, you can't escape you.

The truth is painful but living a lie is torture, for it causes you to enter into a continual losing battle with yourself. #HealingInTruth

The imagination of a child is limitless but the dreams of a broken person are limited. Begin to dream again & work to repair the brokenness.

A true friend loves when it hurts and will celebrate your success in the midst of their own failure. There's no competition among friends.

We must shift our perspective in an effort to obtain the things which we desire. Often times our dreams are deferred because we lose hope.

Luck is based on random occurrences. God doesn't subscribe to this ideology. God always wins. Don't base your life on chance. #LuckRunsOut

In life, we face many challenges and sometimes our faith wavers when times are difficult. But His love for us never wavers. #HisLoveDelivers

I can't move because I refuse to move without God's command. Every time I attempt to move without God, I stumble and fall. #IMoveWhenHeMoves

People have a right to believe what they desire. Typically, people's beliefs don't change. How long will you focus your energy on others?

Are you prepared to do what it takes to get to where you want to go or will you continue to make excuses? Get moving toward your destiny!

You can try to gain the support of many, only to
learn the difficulty in gaining the support of a few.
#UnselfishSupportComesInFewNumbers

For many the greatest test of faith is the ability to trust God
when your current reality contradicts His promise and you're
forced to wait.

Your goal in your personal or professional life should never be
to become someone you're not because being yourself is the best
option.

If people truly knew the struggles and sacrifices of success,
they would learn to appreciate those who have acquired it.
#ThePriceOfSuccess

To support someone because you have a direct benefit is not
support at all, but represents your selfish nature and your insincere motives.

Your enemy is compelled to peek inside the windows of your
life but is angered by what he sees. Keep the curtains open!
#BlindingPresence

You saw me at my lowest and you celebrated. You saw me at
my highest and you were infuriated. I saw your envy and I left.
#EnvyNeverWins

The price of success is great. The cost of unresolved failure is greater. Successful people learn from mistakes.
#TakeFailureOffAutoRepeat

God selects from what is seemingly worthless to others, like out-
casts & the lowly. His goal is to showcase diamonds in the ruff.
#Shine

I listened and all I heard was I. I asked questions and all you said was I. I left and you said I. There is no I in us. #HumilityNotPride

If you desire to receive God's blessings, you must welcome His process. While the process is painful, it's worth the wait. #EndureTheProcess

Isolated pain should lead to our total dependence on God and represent our obedience through suffering. He blesses us through our trials.

You can't lip-sync all your life. At some point the track will skip. Find confidence in your own voice. You can't fake the music! #BeInSync

Successful people perform a risk analysis for those who they allow in their inner circle, as failure to do so can lead to destruction.

Don't confuse intelligence with arrogance, or ignorance for stupidity. Don't confuse being someone else with being you. #SeekClarity

Don't allow your intelligence to turn into arrogance. You will learn knowledge isn't there for you to gain superiority but to inform others.

Temporary fixes can have lifelong consequences. Pain can't be erased with guilt, shame, or abuse. You must deal with it responsibly. #NoPain

It is okay to be patient, pragmatic, and purposeful as you pursue your dreams but don't use the shortcut of conformity to reach your dreams.

My Tweets to You

People who desire to help are often not asked, told, or persuaded but sense a need and quickly attempt to provide without being noticed.

Those who are for you grieve with you, but those who are against you celebrate your grief. Be wise and surround yourself with your allies.

Do not allow your best years to be behind you. Learn to enjoy each phase of your life. We only have this moment! #PressPlayMoveForward

God gives us a blank canvas, but instead of painting a self-portrait, we focus on others. Use the brush on yourself to create a masterpiece.

Many people's inclination is to be dishonest rather than truthful. Truth takes accountability and change. #TruthOverLies

Some people will never have the capacity to support your success because they can't see past their own failure. Envy is an emotion of pain!

Competition at the highest level is based on talent & perseverance. Enemies be aware: there is no competition between us— you're a bystander.

To be average takes some effort and the rewards are few. To be great takes extreme effort but the rewards are plentiful. #DiligentGreatness

The enemy will get in bed with you if you feed them. Your kindness does not change their hatred or motives! #StealKillDestroy

To receive God's blessings, you must believe in yourself.
When you don't have confidence, you tie God's hands!
#ConfidentMeMiraculousGod

God hears all prayers and our selfish desires but He is reluctant
to answer because He understands your heart. Do you pray to
get or give?

Learn to stay closer to God than to your enemies. It's easier for
Satan to attack those who stray away from God. He protects you.
#StayClose

If you truly interrogated your success, you'd understand God
was always with you, even when you contemplated quitting. Success perseveres!

Will you wait for the blessing God has
for you or will you give up prematurely?
#ImpatienceBlocksBlessings #FaithUnleashesBlessings

Revitalization comes when you surrender to God, for you understand your efforts aren't enough. Allow Him to create a new life
of excellence.

When we wait on the Lord, He gives us a reward of abundance.
No matter the depth of our circumstances, He will provide.
#WaitWatchWitnessWin

Fear keeps you in bondage to your past, but courage allows you
to move forward to unlock your future. The key to freedom lies
in your faith!

To believe that true love is an illusion is delusional. To have love,
you must be willing to give love. #GodIsLove #GodIsInUs
#WeAreLove

My Tweets to You

Our peace isn't linked to financial success, but to our Savior. Peace can't be purchased, for God already paid the price. #HeCalmsTheStorm

Fakeness is just like Novocain, as it eventually wears off and you are forced to deal with the realities of your pain. #FakeYouFaceYouFixIt

Helping others is costly and you must count the cost, but turning a blind eye towards those in need has a cost too great for you to pay.

It's okay not to know, but to pretend to know disrupts your ability to seek the truth. Lies are confined! Truth is freedom! God is true!

You can choose to be around takers without talent, or givers with greatness and no envy. The people around you indicate how far you can go!

Your enemies see your greatness as a threat to their mediocrity but God sees you as His prodigy.

If you want to minimize the drama in your life you must no longer produce, promote, and pay for the production. #LiveInPeace #NoMoreDrama

A ferris wheel mentality is content with the mundane, but a roller coaster mentality desires to soar to greater heights. Choose your ride!

To have something useful to say is better than having nothing to say and being useless. We all have value! #LookInward #LoveWithoutEnvy

God isn't concerned about your ability to finish but your inability to be obedient and start. He's the ultimate finisher! #StartNowNoExcuses

What happens when you can't make excuses for someone anymore? #TheirTimeIsUp

If you desire for God to score a touchdown for you, then you must be willing to pass Him the ball. #MeetHimInTheEndzone

You can be a winner and have a losing moment or you can be a loser and have a winning moment. #BeAWinner

Confidence doesn't have to speak. Fakeness does. #SilentConfidence

While there are countless options for excuses, there are simply no substitutions for hard work.

You can either add value or sustain it, but I refuse to let you decrease my value. Wise people know when to walk away. #ValueDriven

Victory has come only because my FAITH was greater than my fear. #FearlessFaith

An oxymoron is a contradiction of terms, like cruel kindness or loving enemy. But is our trust in the Lord an oxymoron? #FaithlessBeliever

A map is meaningless to someone who desires to be lost. Every day we have a choice on the direction we take. #Recalculating #NavigateWithGod

Since when is being positive negative? Life has many curve balls. Nevertheless, my striking out doesn't negate the fact I'm in the game.

King Herod gave orders to kill all boys two years old and younger. It's not you they're after; it's your potential. #JesusTheChild

It takes more energy to swing and miss than it does to swing and connect. Allow God to throw your punches. #GodWinnerByKnockOut

I came; I saw; I conquered. I refused to go; I refused to see; I am defeated. What will be your mantra? I choose God, for He conquers ALL.

Life can back us into a corner with no options. When our strength is gone, He is the source of our strength. Allow Him to fight. #UnDefeated

Life is like a chess game and while our moves are limited, His moves are limitless. Trust that He will make the next move and be victorious!

Negative people have limited vision. To share your dreams with those who can't see beyond their circumstances is a gross waste of your time.

When God implants a vision into your mind & you work to achieve it, some might not understand how it all happened but it's not their vision.

It's important to know that when you can't accomplish something it might not be due to a lack of talent or effort but it's not time. #HoldOn

Negativity impedes success, for it surrenders to all the chatter that says you can't succeed. Positivity tirelessly works for the one YES!

Those who are blessed treat others as God intends them to be treated, not how they deserve to be treated. Love your enemies and be blessed!

As humans, we need nutrients to fuel our bodies. As Christians, we need peace to fuel our soul. #BadFoodHurtsTheBodyBadPeopleHurtTheSoul

There are two types of people: builders and beneficiaries. True friends are excited to help you build, while beneficiaries are opportunists.

If you don't embrace your pain, it will consume you. Don't concede to your sorrow but ask God for peace through your storm. #PeaceBeStill

Life is inherent with unforeseen events. While grass fades & a beautiful rose withers, God's love is unchanged. Exalt God, not your problem.

Your first response in a crisis can have the potential to save your life. We must have a posture of faith, for it determines our response.

Some people believe worrying is a natural emotion but spiritually worrying is habitual. As Christians, we must cast worry aside. #HeCan

A chance to make a difference always starts and ends with you. Don't stagnate making a difference by doing nothing. Be a champion of change!

Fear is an emotion triggered by a perceived threat. Eliminating fear opens the door of opportunity. Don't allow fear to impede your success.

Life is full of possibilities, but the only way to experience them is by using the unlocking mechanism of confidence. I am who I say I am.

A Crisis Christian only has the potential to get out of a particular situation, but a Reflective Christian can navigate all situations.

When God is playing defense for you, rest assured your enemies can never touch you. Many of our blessings are due to His blocking ability.

Prepare yourself to hear "no", to feel disappointment, and ultimately be rejected. Successful people persevere and silence the naysayers.

Character is not what you see when the cameras are rolling, it's what you develop in the darkness. Don't allow poor decisions to expose you!

Success is inherent with many pressures but your character must always be considered your greatest accomplishment. Sacrificing it is failure

Never become so comfortable in your success that you compromise your integrity.

Are there no opportunities in your life? Some people have an inability to see an opportunity as such. You can't seize what you can't see.

What is major? What is minor? Don't lose focus by exhausting your efforts on the minor. Your major objective is to fulfill your purpose.

Great values aren't based on your locality. Your locality isn't an excuse for failure. Your success is based on how you navigate. #Improvise

If you desire to evaluate your inner circle, you must leave it. If in the separation you aren't lacking, then change the people around you.

It is in our darkest hour that our faith must be the strongest because it represents our trust in the Lord. #HeWillNotLeaveOrForsakeYou

Your response to the circumstances of life is a great indication of your ability to succeed. Perseverance is greater than failure.

Waiting a prolonged period of time for your dreams to materialize might be frustrating but God uses our waiting to increase our vision.

Successful people don't only focus on their accomplishments but also on the embedded lessons, which prepare them for future success. Learn!

Acknowledge who sits at the head of the table. Be still. Be Humble. Be thankful. Be love. He is always with you. He is the teacher. #LISTEN

A great representation of your faith lies on the foundation, which you build your vision, character, and truth. Hint: God is Indestructible.

Embrace your truest self, as God has implanted greatness within you. Believe God and become the person you have been created to become.

Dream as big as you can possibly imagine. Silence those who can't see your vision by working until your dream materializes. #IDreamGreatness

Where you are and who you are can be a major contradiction. Don't allow your circumstances to distract you from reaching your destiny.

Fallacy lies in those who see you only for your circumstances or solely for your success, but truth is embedded in your journey. #EmbraceIt

Focusing on the 1% to justify the 99% is not logical. My making it doesn't explain why others didn't. Equality is holistic.

A composite sketch is a reflection of how others see you. The mirror is how you see yourself. God's perception matters the most. #Priceless

There is no mental realm or physical space where you can escape the presence of God. Even in your darkest moments, He is there saying I am.

Many people would prefer to have more resources but before an increase materializes, you must learn how to manage your current inventory.

Be aware your enemies are fully invested in the hope you quit prematurely and never reach your potential. Destroy negativity and persevere!

Don't suppress your emotions. Cry if needed, but don't allow a temporary reality to negate your destiny of greatness.

If your bad habit is not finishing what you start, then you must challenge yourself to move beyond failure and seek completion. #EndureToWin

The concept of change is a fad. The reality of change demands a constant effort. While change can be difficult, it is necessary for growth.

A lie has a false sense of power, for it seems to provide an escape. Only truth has power. If you desire it, you must be willing to change.

You can wait for an opportunity or you can create one. Work until you've utilized all your options then work some more. #BeDeligentBeStrong

Allow your word to mean more than the opinion of others, for it is your virtue, character, integrity, and honesty which indicate your worth

The power of belief and voice are essential to your success. You must believe you are more than average and speak greatness into your life.

Don't disqualify your destiny by allowing others to define you. Be the person God has called you to be, and disregard those who disapprove.

Make no apologies for being great. Make no excuses for failure. Make no room for the past. Make your critics your motivation. Make history!

Success is committed to the finish. The finish is where you display humility knowing your commitment was not in vain. #FinishStrongWin

Do you have the capacity to receive what your heart desires? Wanting something but not being able to sustain it is fool hearted. Be Ready

We live in world where corruption is breaking news, but the millions of children receiving poor education is the real heartbreaking news!

I attempted to be silent, but how does my silence help? The truth cannot be caged or muted. At some point, you must speak the uncomfortable.

People can be judgmental, critical, and even cynical. The key is to not take it personally, but decipher what if any of it is useful.

Our performance is driven by our passion but how do we develop it? Discover your purpose & you will have the passion to perform. #BeOfPurpose

If you refuse to change, understand tomorrow doesn't get better but in some cases it gets worse. Live with purpose, not just for the moment.

A key to success is to surround yourself with people who believe in you for unselfish reasons. The goal is to make you better not to benefit!

A child says to their father, "Your love, strength, resolve, character, voice, and even your walk I aspire to emulate."

Too many children say Happy Father's Day to their mothers. This speaks to dysfunction. A child needs a father's love.

Your enemy is only loyal to your defeat.

Our opportunities indicate how much effort we demonstrate. If you desire a multitude, you must increase your efforts.

As a plane ascends, even the tallest skyscraper becomes minuscule. If you desire to be better, ascend higher than your circumstances.

What happens when you live beneath your potential? You limit your possibilities and live for nothing greater than your limited perspective.

Exposure is to greatness as life is to living. If you desire greatness, it is imperative you step outside of your comfort zone.

The enemy will RSVP to your party but don't be dismayed. Be thankful to God for sending the invitation. He will bless you in their presence.

Our subconscious mind must be in agreement with our conscious mind. Internal is thinking and external is speaking. #ThoughtsWinWordsLose

We can emulate the behavior of someone else, only to discover the outcome is not what we expected. Focus only on your talent and perfect it.

Contrast provides perspective. Be thankful for your trials. It is in those realities that you find the greatest joy, knowing you overcame.

Bitterness and blame do not heal your pain but keep you at a constant level of discomfort. Forgiveness allows you to move on and heal.

Looking back over one's life exposes one fundamental truth, which is we have no control of life's obstacles. We only control our reactions.

Our thoughts become our life's forecast. We must change how we think in an effort to change what we do. We are products of our thoughts.

A broken heart or a shattered dream is the perfect canvas for God, for His work always becomes a masterpiece. The mirror reveals His work.

Your life is a gift. If you choose to give it to someone who is unappreciative & undeserving, be prepared to deal with unnecessary pain.

Instead of seeking someone to make you happy, perhaps you need to improve your life & find contentment, & someone can join your happiness.

Most of us can look in the mirror and utter the phrase, "I haven't done my best." Accountability comes before blame. Better is the goal.

It's imperative to find contentment with those things you'll likely never understand because if you don't, you become broken and resentful.

We must stop comparing, critiquing, and envying others, as it disrupts our focus. The desire to be someone else is unrealistic. #FocusOnYou

It isn't wise to be arrogant, but it's foolish to lack confidence. Confidence births greatness and delivers opportunity. You're good enough!

When you choose to play down your success to make others comfortable be aware that in the end, you will feel the most discomfort.

Success interrogates the obvious, displays passion, thinks beyond potential and eliminates excuses. Success is not meant to be easy, people!

You can easily spend your entire life focused on others or you can choose to live, not just be alive. Regret is painful and time escapes us.

Each day we make history, most which will be untold. But if you desire to make history which lasts, become fearless & unwavering. #Victory

If your logic is based on rationalized stupidity and sophisticated ignorance, chances are you're allergic to the truth. #SeekTruthAndBeWell

Seize the moment and cherish it but don't take for granted the effects it will have on tomorrow. Success comes with great responsibility.

Sometimes life will give you exactly what you desire. It is imperative you be prepared before you ask. Be appreciative and sustain the gift!

People chasers are most concerned about the opinions of others. However, purpose chasers are most concerned about becoming their best.

Life is a stage. Each character has a purpose. We must learn to embrace our roles with intensity and integrity.

It's foolish to believe having goals alone will place you on the road to success. The fact is a goal without planning & hard work is a wish.

If all you do is walk out the door and deliver a fake image to the world, chances are you're running from yourself. Face your truth. Change!

My Tweets to You

How you carry yourself gives a better glimpse into your life than your resume does. Greatness is a demonstration, not self-proclaimed talk.

Mediocrity has no credence! For some, it seemingly paves the way, but is incapable of allowing you to be great. #StriveForGreatness

In life, we have to let the song play, for when it stops we have to decide if it should be added to the soundtrack of life. #EditWisely

Intentionality doesn't negate or minimize the consequences of poor decisions. Beyond being apologetic, what action are you taking to change?

If your relationships are in shambles, you must interrogate your relationship with God. Loving humanity more than God leads to destruction!

It is rare to have no fault in a situation. But in reality, many people lack accountability because accepting fault leads to correction.

Within your circumstances lie two distinct paths. One is defined by the situation and the other is based on you redefining the situation.

Some people believe that success requires little change but in an effort to be successful, you must eliminate excuses and change as needed.

It's called selective hearing, selective amnesia, and selective vision. How can you change what you refuse to hear, remember, or see?

Set realistic goals. Understand it only takes one yes. Be dedicated to your goals and take ownership of your failure. #AccountabilityIsAMust

An "IF" mentality feeds off worry, anxiety, and stress. We have no control of what will happen in our lives. We only control our decisions.

There is no point to being negative. Use your energy to be positive despite the situation. It is in our reactions that we find regret.

As youngsters, we claim to have many friends but as we become older, we soon realize true friends are rare. True friends are gifts from God!

We must learn to manage our obligations by not trying to do more than we can handle. Overload, anxiety, and stress impede success. #RestToWin

To relocate is tough & erupts a great deal of emotions but to stay past your time in any particular space or with a person robs you of time.

A true friend is never intimidated by your questions but listens with intensity to understand how they can help. Your enemy listens to hurt.

The devastation is upon us and we see the destruction. The families of Oklahoma must know that God is with them to turn tragedy into love.

Self-reliance is great but shouldn't turn into stubbornness. We all need help sometimes. Those who are afraid to seek it lose by technicality.

My Tweets to You

Our faith must always include love, for love forgives, doesn't judge or account wrongs, and sees the best in others. We need FAITH and LOVE!

You will always fall short of your potential when you fail to listen.

The mirror reinforces vanity but isn't capable of hiding the truth. Despite efforts to live outside of reality, the mirror says change now!

We must become contributors to humanity & allow our lives to transform future generations. Your labor will not be in vain when you persist.

Success requires discipline. How can you desire the best but not give it? For most of us, it's not lack of talent but lack of discipline.

I wanted to take you with me but you fought every step of the way. Now it's time to travel to my destiny alone. True love has no prisoners.

We are products of our thoughts. Change your thinking and you can transform your life. Exposure is everything. #GreatnessSeeksGreatness

Unfortunately envy & jealously don't present themselves in certain terms. Sometimes our greatest enemies are those we perceive as friends.

If you're around people who're always in awe of you, chances are you have fans, not friends. A fan consumes talent. A friend adds to it.

We must make a conscious effort to see the good in all things, for if we don't we'll be consumed by our trials. The reality is life happens.

We should not solely define ourselves by success or talent but by how we utilize our success and talent to shape others. Share your gifts!

We have more commonalities than we have differences. We must learn to embrace humanity and focus on what unites us. Become the collective.

We start many things. Perhaps you started a remodeling project or began to read a book. Starting isn't the goal—finishing is. Persistence!

Parenting is one of the most difficult responsibilities. While each parent plays a pivotal role, a mother is priceless.

You can spend your life chasing things money can buy, only to discover time, joy, peace, love, and happiness are NotForSale. #MoneyHasLimits

Our lives must be impregnated with passion and nurtured with love so we can birth greatness into the world.

The fear to succeed is the fuel needed for failure. What if Edison gave in to fear? Be bold and watch the lights of success guide your path!

Even in the face of disappointment, you must strive toward your goal. No is only final when you concede. The lesson is in the NO!

Someone in the distance yells stop but you keep going. Sirens are approaching but you fail to yield. Hearing is not enough. Hear to respond!

One of the greatest tragedies is to die not knowing why you lived. Live with purpose. For God so loved the world, He created you!

If you have a total disregard for truth, knowledge, and understanding chances are, your life will be chaotic due to a lack of wisdom.

If you have a great idea or concept, spend less time gaining consensus or validation and more time on implementation. Be Confident

There is a difference between admiration and imitation. Be original. Be you!

If you travel to the ends of earth, you would discover we all have issues but those who persevere understand God is greater than our issues.

Don't only be impressed with a person's current accomplishments, for oftentimes the greater story is captured in their journey.

Oftentimes the greatest obstacle you will face is yourself.

Having faith at the finish line is not a great demonstration of faith. Learn to have faith before your dreams materialize. #TrustGodBelieve

All across the nation students will graduate. I pray they use their education as a means to transform. We salute your tenacity to finish.

Sarcasm speaks without love. Ridicule speaks without a filter. Envy speaks without happiness. Truth speaks without excuses.

What we say perhaps has already been said and what we do has probably already been done. So where do we go from here? Just be yourself.

Maybe you had a rough childhood or you're dealing with residual pain. But as long as you choose to rest in pain, you will never find peace.

Yes I am tired. Giving up is easy. Success is never achieved by those who lack endurance but by those who pressed forward. Be Resilient!

Your profession or craft is often judged by results but your work ethic is judged by your effort and character. Work hard and with purpose.

What you do is okay, given you can handle the critique and or consequence.

We need to stop educating that entertainment is a way out, and entertain the ways education can change where you are. Education transforms.

Dream above the rim, wider than the field, bigger than the silver screen and louder than the music. With God, our possibilities are endless!

Life is about perspective. How you view your circumstances determines how you navigate the situation. Be positive!

Life is about purpose. When you know your talents, you can live within your gifts and not envy others. Be yourself!

Life is about decisions. The better decisions you make, the better life you will be afforded. Be wise in your decision making.

Mistakes can be instantaneous but correcting those mistakes can take a lifetime. Don't waste time making foolish mistakes.

Ignorance does not grant you a pass when you make a mistake but sometimes we find ourselves spending a lifetime trying to right our wrongs.

Your responsibilities speak to your level of success. If you spend the day doing trivial things, chances are success is not your goal.

Learn the WHY and then spend your life doing WHAT needs to be done. Living your life in the HOW, WHEN, and WHO stops progress. Ready Set GO!

To measure a person's character, we must look outside their families and see how their life has impacted others. Learn to give beyond self!

You can choose to avoid responsibilities, but understand indecision and irresponsibility are in fact decisions. Decisions have implications.

People fear change but change is often a sign of growth. If you desire to grow and be better learn to embrace change. Don't fail to change!

Time cannot be purchased. There is no 401K for time. The reality is time is running out. Make your seconds count. Before your time is up!

Allow God to be the author of your narrative, for if you take the pen, you will be forced to detour from His plan. Who desires to be lost?

Don't bypass the NOW! Live in the moment for it is where opportunity lives. Do your very best in the moment and the future will make itself!

Love is an abstract concept but it is also a demonstration. Those who truly love you understand the word is meaningless without action.

You can't make ready wait.

When opportunities arise, we must seize them. However, opportunities are useless if we are ill prepared. Be Ready! Be Focused! Be You!

It is easy to focus on those who made it but why are there so many who don't? Perhaps poverty is more dehumanizing than we'd like to admit.

Choice matters! We need more options for schools. What parent wants their child to attend a failing school? More options more opportunities.

Understanding who you are is far more valuable than making sense of others. Invest in yourself, as it is the only way to help others.

Distractions can be deadly. Your focus matters. Once we lose focus, we lack direction and allow our circumstances to determine our destiny.

A rose in the concrete is just as beautiful as a rose in the garden. Don't allow your position to determine your worth. Believe in yourself!

Today the sun is shining but somewhere else, there is a storm. Don't allow the weather to determine your mood. Isn't your presence enough?

Living in the past doesn't change the realities of today or the future. Stop rereading old chapters of your life. Next Chapter Please!

Desire, Dedication, and Determination lead to success. Apathy, indifference, and indecision lead to failure. Choose your path wisely.

Children are our future. Yet many receive a poor education, live in poverty, and die by violence. We must invest in the future! NOW!

Those who truly desire to change are open to critical feedback but those who aren't despise the truth, doing little to change their reality.

Wanting people to listen to your problems is noble but listening alone doesn't resolve issues. A byproduct of love is correction and action.

Love can't be purchased or bartered but must be freely given. Those who receive it shouldn't take it for granted, as it will be taken away!

May God be with the families of Boston, for it's in tragedy we learn the power of His peace. May His love and grace be our protection. Amen!

Complaining does nothing to change your circumstances. Instead of being bitter, make an effort to correct the mistakes you made.

Being smart isn't being lame. However being lazy, unmotivated and complacent isn't being smart. Your life's result is based on your efforts.

Life has swift transitions, but those who can withstand them are those who understand the transitions were only temporary. Learn to live.

Its takes effort to learn and live in greatness.

Mediocrity lacks purpose and complacency lacks change. Our greatest weakness is our inability to look inward and rewrite our truths.

Through the miraculous power of God, coupled with our demonstration of faith, we have the power to transform our dreams into reality.

We must become the change we hope to see. Do not consume yourself with things you cannot change.

Instead of dealing with our issues, we often focus on others.

Victims become prisoners of their pain. If you desire freedom, you must allow God to be bigger than your circumstances. Become victorious.

A recurring theme in life is yourself. Refuse to have a victim mentality. Take accountability for your life and make changes when needed.

When opportunity presents itself people will show what they always wanted to do and unfortunately, some will do nothing.

Opportunity has the ability to reveal your true character. You either will be a person of action or complacency.

Only truth brings ultimate clarity and you must make a conscious decision to walk in your truth.

People who are successful often hear no. They refuse to allow it to become a defining mantra, but persevere until their dream materializes.

Understanding what needs to be done and doing what must be done are two different tracks. You must move from understanding to action.

Never stop dreaming, but chase your dreams with such fervor that in the end you are not the only one impressed with the results.

Learning to forgive is less consuming than holding on to unresolved pain and resentment.

The only power you possess is the power to change yourself.

If you are reading these closing words perhaps you have completed the entire book or you just decided to read ahead but either way the purpose of the book was for you to find a Tweet or Tweets that speak directly to you. If you found that particular Tweet or Tweets then my job here is done but your job is not complete until you have shared what you have learned.

LIFE TO LEGACY LLC

Let us bring your story to life! Life to Legacy offers the following publishing services: manuscript development, editing, transcription services, ghostwriting, cover design, copyright services, ISBN assignment, worldwide distribution, and eBooks.

Throughout the entire production process, you maintain control over your project. Even if you have no manuscript, we can ghostwrite your story for you from audio recordings or legible handwritten documents. Whether print-on-demand or trade publishing, we have publishing packages to meet your needs. We make the production and publishing processes easy for you.

We also specialize in family history books, so you can leave a written legacy for your children, grandchildren, and others. You put your story in our hands, and we'll bring it to literary life!

Please visit our website:
www.Life2Legacy.com

Or call us at:
877-267-7477

You can also e-mail us at:
Life2Legacybooks@att.net

www.ingramcontent.com/pod-product-compliance
Lightning Source LLC
Chambersburg PA
CBHW021337090426
42742CB00008B/633